MW01267722

PUBLISHED FOR THE MALONE SOCIETY
BY MANCHESTER UNIVERSITY PRESS

Oxford Road, Manchester M13 9NR, UK
and Room 400, 175 Fifth Avenue, New York, NY 10010, USA
www.manchesteruniversitypress.co.uk

Distributed exclusively in the USA by
Palgrave, 175 Fifth Avenue, New York,
NY 10010, USA

Distributed exclusively in Canada by
UBC Press, University of British Columbia, 2029 West Mall,
Vancouver, BC, Canada V6T 1Z2

British Library Cataloguing-in-Publication Data
A catalogue record for this book is available from the British Library

Library of Congress Cataloging-in-Publication Data applied for

ISBN 978 0 7190 8096 8

Typeset by New Leaf Design, Scarborough, North Yorkshire
Printed by Henry Ling Limited, at the Dorset Press, Dorchester, DT1 1HD

THE TRIAL OF TREASURE

THE MALONE SOCIETY
REPRINTS, VOL. 173
2008 (2010)

This edition of *The Trial of Treasure* has been prepared by Peter Happé and checked by John Jowett, G. R. Proudfoot, and H. R. Woudhuysen.

December 2009   JOHN JOWETT

INTRODUCTION

The Trial of Treasure was printed by Thomas Purfoote, senior, with the date 1567 on its title page.[1] Because it appeared at a time when interludes had become very common in print and performance and because it shares a number of concepts and devices with other similar extant plays there is no reason to suppose that it was composed earlier than the 1560s. Though many books printed by Purfoote were entered in the Stationers' Register at this time and though he himself occasionally held office for the Company, this play is not recorded.

The text is printed in quarto in five quires, collating 4°, A–D⁴ E⁶, A, B, D, and E being signed i–iii, and C i–ii.[2] The title page (A1ʳ) gives Purfoote's address in St Paul's Churchyard. The verso (A1ᵛ) has Purfoote's large pictorial device of a Lucrece (i.e. Lucretia) with THOMAS PURFOOTE on the label below.[3] A preliminary poem on A2ʳ⁻ᵛ (the speaker of which is referred to on the title page as '[the] Preface' rather than a prologue) begins with a two-line ornamental capital D. The text begins, on A3ʳ, with a two-line capital H and runs to E4ᵛ ('Finis.'). This is followed by a versified prayer 'for all estates', beginning with a two-line roman capital T, and ending with 'Finis.' (E5ʳ). The last printed page has the Lucrece device once more, together with a colophon repeating Purfoote's address on three lines, but without the date (E5ᵛ). E6, where it survives, is blank.

The following five copies have been collated for this edition:

British Library (C.34.b.49; cropped, wants E3–4 and E6) [BL];
Bodleian Library (Malone 231(4); cropped, wants E5–6) [BOD];
Huntington Library (69673; slightly cropped, wants E5) [HN];

---

[1] *A Short-title Catalogue of Books printed in England, Scotland and Ireland and of English Books printed abroad, 1475–1640*, compiled by A. W. Pollard and G. R. Redgrave, 2nd edn. revised and enlarged by W. A. Jackson, F. S. Ferguson and Katharine F. Pantzer, 3 vols. (London: Bibliographical Society, 1976–91), no. 24271; W. W. Greg, *A Bibliography of the English Printed Drama to the Restoration*, 4 vols. (London: Bibliographical Society, 1939–59), no. 49.

[2] This collation is somewhat conjectural in respect of E, depending upon consideration of chain lines and watermarks below pp. ix–x.

[3] R. B. McKerrow, *Title-page Borders used in England and Scotland, 1485–1640* (London: Bibliographical Society, 1932), no. 151.

Harry Ransom Library, Austin, Texas (Pforz 524; perfect) [TEX]; from the Mostyn sale[4] via the Pforzheim collection. This is the text reproduced in the present facsimile.[5]

Rosenbach Library, Philadelphia (EL1.altr; wants E6) [ROS]; formerly owned by W. A. White and part of the Irish Find.[6]

The play is faintly traceable in the late seventeenth century. Kirkman lists it (1661), but Langbaine (1691), though he mentions the title, says he is a stranger to it. Later on Baker gives the title page but no further details (1782).[7]

The extended collation of copies undertaken for this edition has enabled a clearer perception of the text to emerge than that in the analysis by W. W. Greg, based only upon the defective BL and BOD copies, in which he attempted conjecturally to reconstruct the E quire.[8] His conclusion, that the surviving copies give evidence for only one edition, has been sustained by the current investigation, especially by consideration of the inking process mentioned below. As we shall see, there is some indication that two compositors may have worked on the text, one on quires A and B, and another on parts of the rest. The evidence for such a possibility arises from differences in convention for catchwords, in ways of setting out stage directions, in the incidence of lower case letters at the beginning of lines, the use of pilcrows, the occurrence of commas at ends of speeches, in addition to the absence of a signature on C3^r and the apparent errors on C3^v. Though alternative explanations for some of these features may call such a conclusion into question, cumulatively they suggest that it cannot be entirely dismissed.

Three later editions have also been consulted:

(1) James Orchard Halliwell, *The Interlude of the Trial of Treasure: Reprinted from the black-letter edition by Thomas Purfoote* (London: Percy

---

[4] Books belonging to Lord Mostyn of Mostyn Hall were sold at Sotheby's on 20–1 March 1919: *A Catalogue of a most important and interesting collection of Early English Plays* (London: Sotheby, Wilkinson and Hodges, 1919).

[5] The Malone Society regrets that photographer's clamps are visible at the top of some pages.

[6] According to the prefatory note (pages not numbered) in J. S. Farmer (ed.), *King Darius: An Hitherto Unknown Edition*, Tudor Facsimile Texts (London: T. C. and E. C. Jack, 1907) 'three plays supposedly lost' were found in an Irish country house in 1906 and sold at Sotheby's in the same year.

[7] Francis Kirkman, *A True perfect and exact catalogue of all the Comedies, Tragedies and Tragi-Comedies, Pastorals, Masques and Interludes that were ever yet printed and published till this present year, 1661* (London: Brook, *et al.*, 1661), p. 554; Gerard Langbaine, *An Account of the English dramatick poets* (Oxford: L. L. for G. West and H. Clements, 1691), B4; David Erskine Baker, *Biographica Dramatica, or, A companion to the playhouse*, 2nd edn. Supplemented by Isaac Reed, 2 vols. (London, 1782), ii. 382.

[8] W. W. Greg, 'The Trial of Treasure, 1567.—A Study in Ghosts', *The Library*, Third Series, 1 (1910), 28–35.

vi

Society, 1850). This edition is close to the original in spelling, but W. W. Greg showed that it was in fact derived from a faulty transcript of BOD (British Library MS Royal 298),[9] thus refuting Halliwell's proposal, based on the transcript, that there were two editions.

(2) Robert Dodsley, *A Select Collection of Old English Plays*, fourth edition revised by William Carew Hazlitt (London: Reeves and Turner, 1874–6), vol. 1. This edition is in modernized spelling and it has been edited in respect of punctuation.

(3) John S. Farmer, *Anonymous Plays* (Third Series), reprint (New York: Barnes and Noble, 1966): modernized and annotated.

THOMAS PURFOOTE AS PRINTER

Thomas Purfoote was active as a printer and bookseller from 1546 to 1605, by which time his son, also Thomas, had taken over the business. During the father's long career we find over 170 titles attributed to him in *STC*. About five of his books per year have survived from the 1560s, but the number of surviving titles increases markedly for later years, reaching over ten titles in 1583 and 1586. For the year 22 July 1565 to 22 July 1566 the Stationers' Register records thirteen titles in his name, and for the following twelve months the total is ten.[10] In 1567 his shop was in St Paul's churchyard, where he traded from about 1550 until 1577 at the sign of Lucrece.[11]

This shop sign no doubt relates to the woodcut we have noted on A1[v] and E5[v].[12] The latter also appears on the verso of the title leaf in Sir David Lindsay, *A dialogue betweene Experience and a Courtier* (1566: STC 15676; 4°);[13] and in a similar position in W. Fulke, *Praelections vpon the sacred and holy Reuelation of S. John* (1573: STC 11443 4°).[14] A smaller version of the Lucrece with LUCRECIA ROMANA [N turned] on the label (McKerrow, no. 161) came into use by the Purfootes later, as in Lewis Evans, *The hatefull hypocrisie, and rebellion of the Romishe prelacie* (1570: STC 10591, 8°) and Humphrey Baker, *The well spring of sciences* (1612: STC 1216, 8°), printed by Purfoote junior. A third version in an oval (McKerrow, no. 173) appears in his edition of Antonio di Corro, *Dialogus theologicus . . . Pauli ad*

[9] Ibid., 32–4.
[10] Edward Arber, *A Transcript of the Registers of the Company of Stationers of London, 1554–1640 AD*, 5 vols. (London: privately printed, 1875–94), pp. 127–56.
[11] E. G. Duff, *A Century of the English Book Trade* (London: Bibliographical Society, 1905), pp. 125–6.
[12] See n. 3 above.
[13] Two copies in Cambridge University Library: Pet. Sp 79; Syn.7.56.40[1].
[14] Copies in the British Library and the Bodleian.

Romanos (1574: STC 5784) and C. Desainliens, *The Italian schoole-maister* (1608: STC 6760), printed by his son.[15]

Purfoote printed books of many different kinds. There were almanacs and prognostications, and works about sensational subjects such as *A monstrous fishe* (1566: STC 6769) and *A . . . horrible murther . . . nere Roane* (1586: STC 11377). His list included educational works such as short dictionaries, and *An. A.B.C.* (1561: STC 19.4); and a (lost) volume with this seductive title: *A Delysious Surupe newly Claryfied for yonge schollers that thruste [thirst] for the swete lycoure of laten speache.*[16] There were religious works, such as Lewis Evans, *The mysterie of the euchariste* (1569: STC 10593) and Robert Heasse, *A chrystian, exhortation verye profitable gathered out of the holye scriptures* (1565–6: STC 13017), and two commentaries on St Paul's Epistles by Jean Calvin (1581: STC 4401, 4403).[17] The scope of his undertakings could be ambitious, as in the 457-page folio of Petrus Pena and Matthias de L'Obel, *Stirpium aduersaria noua* (1571: STC 19595), a formidable illustrated catalogue of plants. Among literary texts there are many ballads ('balletts'), some about love, and some with a distinctly classical or mythological interest such as *A Ballett entituled An History of Alexander Campaspe and Apelles* (1565–6).[18] A more substantial undertaking in verse was Lindsay, *A dialogue betweene Experience and a Courtier*, which he printed initially with William Pickering and reissued in 1575 and 1581. The title page for the first edition is very similar in layout to *Trial* and the text is in the same size of black letter. There was also a translation from Boccaccio, *Nastagio and Trauersari* (1569: STC 3184). He was thus an experienced printer of verse, especially around the time of the printing of *Trial*.

There are, however, very few indications that he printed plays. Apart from *Trial*, the Stationers' Register records only one text, no longer extant (1566–7):

Received of Thomas Purfoote for his lycense for ye pryntinge of a playe of fortune to knowe eche one of hyr cōdicions genntle manors as well of women as of men &c. . . . iiijd.[19]

Greg attributes two other plays to Purfoote in the year 1605: John Marston, *The Dutch courtezan* (STC 17475), and Thomas Heywood, *If you know not*

---

[15] The title page of *Precationes priuatae* by Elizabeth I (1563: STC 7576.7, 16°) has caryatids at the side together with TP's monograph (R. B. McKerrow, *Printers' and Publishers' Devices in England and Scotland, 1485–1640* (London: Bibliographical Society, 1913), no. 140.

[16] Arber, *Transcript*, vol. 1, p. 188 (1569–70).

[17] As noted below, this interest is matched in *Trial*.

[18] Arber, *Transcript*, vol. 1, p. 137b.

[19] Ibid., p. 150b.

me, you know nobodie, Part 1 (STC 13328).[20] By this date it is likely that the business had been taken over by his son, and the conventions for printing plays had changed considerably. There is, for example, much more systematic attention to punctuation in these texts than in *Trial*, and roman type was used.

PRINTING *THE TRIAL OF TREASURE*, 1567

The text of *Trial* offers a tidy and well-designed appearance and it shows signs of professional competence. It shares many features which had become conventional for the printing of plays by this period.[21] It is printed in black letter throughout, four different sizes being used. The largest, measuring 7 mm, is used on l. 1 of the title page and for initial H on A3^r (Type 1); in the songs lower case 'e' measures 4 mm (Type 2); in the main text, including the speech prefixes in the outer margins, it is 3 mm (Type 3); and in almost all the stage directions 2 mm (Type 4). There are no running heads. The page depth is maintained at 32 lines of Type 3, though there is some variation, when Type 2 occurs (as in A3^r, 29 lines of type) and for Type 4 (as in A4^r, 33 lines of type).

Some watermarks have been found, though specific designs are often hard to determine:

BL: A1:4 (pot?); B2; C2 (possibly the same as in A1:4); D1:4; E1 (top of pot):[6 missing].
BOD: A2:3 (perhaps pointing hand); B2:3 (pot); C2:3 (pointing hand); D4; E1:[6 missing]; E3:E4.
TEX: A1; B4; C2:3 (fingers on C2); D2; E2:E5.
HN: A2:3 (hand and flower); E1 (hand and flower); E6 (hand and flower).
ROS: B2; C3; D4; E1; E2.

Deficiencies in the E quire in four of the five surviving copies may need some explanation. As is apparent from chain lines which correspond on E1 and E6, and from the chain lines and the watermark across the gutter of E2:E5, TEX, the only perfect copy, has conjugacy: E1:E6; E2:E5 and E3:E4. This is partially corroborated by BOD, which lacks E5 and E6. Here the chain lines and the watermark match across the gutter in E3:E4. In this copy there is also half of a pot watermark near the gutter on E1 similar to

[20] Greg, *Bibliography*, nos. 214 and 215.
[21] I have discussed some of these in 'Printers of Interludes', in *A Blackwell Companion to Tudor Literature and Culture, 1485–1603*, edited by Kent Cartwright (Oxford: Blackwell, 2010), pp. 192–210.

that in E3, but the chain lines on E1 do not correspond with those on E4, indicating that in all probability E1 was conjugate with the missing E6. Further support for this explanation comes from HN which has a hand and flower watermark and chain lines pointing to conjugacy of E1:E6. However, there remains some uncertainty about BL where chain lines in E2 and E5 do not appear to match closely across the gutter, leaving it possible that they are disjunct. But this is an isolated anomaly for which other explanations are possible, especially as in this copy the leaves of this half-sheet are not cut accurately. It is likely that originally these pages were conjugate.

The loss of leaves at the back of the volume may have been accidental because they were exposed. But there is also a possibility that the losses in BOD and HN could have resulted from deliberate excision. This may be because the prayer on E5^r or the Lucrece on E5^v attracted attention.[22] The evidence just presented appears to point to a pattern of conjugacy in sheet E unexpected in quarto printing, namely E1:6, E2:5, E3:4. If this is indeed the case, it leaves doubt about the identity of the added bifolium, which must have been printed as a half-sheet, presumably by half-sheet imposition. But the correspondence of chain lines and watermarks we have noted in several copies makes it unlikely that the added half-sheet could have consisted of E5 and E6.

In HN A1 is not conjugate with A4. This may be accounted for by the need to replace a lost title page which was met by incorporating a leaf from another copy now lost.

The quarto is tidy in appearance especially with regard to justification of lines: impressive examples of neat work by a compositor can be seen at B3^r, C1^r, C1^v and C4^v. The most significant feature of this concern is that, in order to avoid verse lines running over, ampersands and letters with tildes or superior abbreviations are used extensively. The distribution of abbreviations by formes is as follows:

[22] If the acts of removing of E5 from BOD and HN were deliberate, and not accidents, there are several possible explanations, but there is no information about when they might have taken place. It is possible that there might have been contemporary or later objections to the prayer (E5^r) on ideological grounds, but equally someone might have wanted to save it positively for other purposes. On the other hand this leaf may have been selected for excision because of the Lucrece (E5^v). This is a duplicate of A1^v and it is thus superfluous, and it happens to be quite an attractive woodcut which someone might want to collect. In any case it is not apparent which of the two sides of this leaf might have been the objective of any of these courses of action and the two acts of removal might have been quite independent of one another. As E6 is blank, it might simply have been convenient to tear it out from BOD along with E5.

	Outer amp.	tilde	y^e	other	Inner amp.	tilde	y^e	other
A	1	5	4		3	9	4	
B	2	8	1		5	5		
C	3	7			1	9	1	
D		4	1	y^t	1	10	7	Tarquini^9 y^t
E	1					1		y^u(2)

In some places punctuation is omitted for the same purpose. There are no stops at the ends of speeches where the line is too long, as at TLN 138, 141, 256, 490, 608, 618, 769, 855, 873 and 878.

The arrangement of speech prefixes shows a similar concern for tidiness. They are usually confined to one line by means of abbreviation and by omitting punctuation. The forms of abbreviation adopted for these prefixes are not consistent, but there is a working limit of a maximum of about 17 mm, effectively seven Type 3 letters and a stop, as in 'Inclina.' (TLN 228). The only exceptions, both on B2ᵛ, are 'Sturdi=/nes.' (TLN 281–2) and 'Inclina=/tion' (298–9). In general speech prefixes appear in the outer margins: on the right for rectos and on the left for versos. Some false alignment, as e.g. at TLN 236–7 (B1ᵛ), 363–5 (B3ᵛ) or 568–94 (C3ʳ), suggests that they were set as separate blocks of type.

The aesthetic concern for a neat appearance may also affect indentation of lines. The normal practice is to indent the start of stanzas (A2ʳ⁻ᵛ, E5ʳ); for subsections of songs (B1ᵛ, B2ᵛ, B4ʳ, C4ʳ, E1ʳ), and the beginning of speeches. It was clearly thought desirable to do this, and it is indeed a practical help to someone reading or acting from a text. But for the beginnings of speeches the practice is changed in the majority of places where the indentation for a single-line speech should be followed immediately by another in the next line. Instead the compositor almost invariably aligns the second speech to the left margin. The effect upon the general appearance is to create an impression of well-arranged blocks of text in units of several lines. A good illustration of this will be found on B3ᵛ where four possible indentations are ignored (TLN 348, 363, 365, 367). It does, however, seem to have been acceptable to indent alternate lines for three or more one-line speeches, as at TLN 265–9. Other factors may also have affected the choice, including lines being too long to indent, which led to the pattern being reversed as at TLN 614–5, 855–7, 873–6 (where 614, 855 and 873 are too long). This leaves three further exceptions. In some places an individual line is too long to indent (TLN 143, 285, 742). In others there is no perceptible reason for the failure to indent, except the possibility of an interest in aesthetic appearance noted above or hasty setting (TLN 97, 772, 853, 919, 929, 931, 935, 1020; 919–35 all occur on D4ᵛ). For two entrances by Inclination there is no speech prefix and the indents alone indicate a new speech (TLN 178, 464).

There are a number of short lines, most of which are indented from the left margin. They usually comprise complete speeches, and occur at TLN 96 (not indented), 253, 267, 277–8 (couplet), 529 (not indented), 609, 618, 825–6 (couplet), 856, 911, 927, 1152 (not indented). The two short lines at TLN 304–5 together make up a single divided verse line which rhymes with 306.

Catchwords appear on every text page except A1^r, A1^v, A2^v, E4^v, E5^r and E5^v. They are aligned right within the main body of the text. They correspond exactly with the first word of all the following pages except in these instances:

Outer

A3^r 𝔖𝔭𝔯 | 𝔏𝔲𝔰𝔱𝔢. 𝔖𝔦𝔯; D1^r 𝔯𝔢𝔠𝔬𝔯𝔡𝔢 | 𝔯𝔢𝔠𝔬𝔯𝔡; D3^r 𝔶𝔬𝔲 | 𝔏𝔲𝔰𝔱𝔢. 𝔜𝔬𝔲; E2^v 𝔄𝔫 | 𝔄𝔫𝔡

Inner

B4^r 𝔒𝔲𝔯 | 𝔈𝔩𝔞𝔱𝔦𝔬𝔫. 𝔒𝔲𝔯; C2^r 𝔄 𝔤𝔞𝔪= | 𝔄 𝔤𝔞𝔪𝔟𝔬𝔩𝔩𝔦𝔫𝔤; C4^r 𝔗𝔥𝔢𝔯= | 𝔗𝔥𝔢𝔯𝔢𝔣𝔬𝔯𝔢; D2^r 𝔣𝔯𝔦𝔢𝔫𝔡= | 𝔣𝔯𝔦𝔢𝔫𝔡𝔰𝔥𝔦𝔭; D4^r 𝔒𝔣 | 𝔍𝔫 𝔩𝔦𝔫𝔞. 𝔒𝔣; E4^r 𝔏𝔢𝔱 | 𝔗𝔯𝔲𝔰𝔱𝔢. 𝔏𝔢𝔱

It will be seen from this that there are apparently errors on D1^r and E2^v. The omission of a speech prefix occurs only on rectos: A3^r, B4^r, D3^r, D4^r, and E4^r. As there are no places where a speech prefix appears in a catch-word, this would seem to be consistent and deliberate, presumably because the speech prefixes were set in a separate column of type as noted above. Abbreviation of long words using = to mark it occurs only on inner-forme pages in a cluster at C2^r, C4^r and D2^r. (and these too are all rectos). By contrast on three other pages a long word is given in full: A4^r '𝔍𝔫𝔬𝔯𝔡𝔦𝔫𝔞𝔱𝔢'; D2^v '𝔗𝔯𝔢𝔞𝔰𝔲𝔯𝔢'; and E1^r '𝔖𝔬𝔪𝔢𝔱𝔦𝔪𝔢'. Another feature is that seven catchwords show irregularities of spacing or horizontal alignment. This may be related to the frequency of uneven spacing between letters in the text itself, as in '𝔥𝔬 𝔴' (TLN 375), '𝔬𝔠 𝔠𝔞𝔰𝔦𝔬𝔫' (450), and '𝔴𝔦𝔩 𝔩' (515). Both probably result from slack locking of the type pages in the chase.

Concern for the appearance of the text may well have taken precedence over punctuation in a number of places. But there is a more general absence of marks where there is no pressure upon space, as well as inconsistent use of full stops and commas. Commas appear at the end of speeches instead of full stops throughout the text in this distribution:

Speeches ending with commas:

	Outer	*Inner*
A		2
B	1	6
C	2	2
D	2	
E	2	1

This substitution tends to occur when there is an exchange of single-line speeches, as at 'Ꞙⁿⁱuaꝑe,' (TLN 89) 'Ꞙtoꝛe,' (404). More strikingly, some stage directions also end with commas, a concentration of these occurring in quire C:

Stage directions ending with commas:

	Outer	Inner
A		1 (in margin)
B		
C	2	7
D	1	1
E	1	2

Lightness of punctuation can leave the reader without useful guidance to understanding the turns of speech, as with the Vice's lines at TLN 464–75. The Vice's long speech at TLN 549–66 has a comma at the end of every line including the last. There is also a paucity of marks of interrogation and exclamation, though some sentence endings are marked appropriately.

The text is exceptionally valuable for its fifty or so stage directions. Their positioning varies, and this may be an indication that some were embedded in the original copy and that others were added to it later. It is desirable to consider first their distribution in relation to the use of pilcrows. The latter are used with discrimination, but we shall see there is a notable variation in practice. Large ones embellish the title page and headings on A2ʳ, A3ʳ and E5ʳ including the first entry of Lust (TLN 60). There is no attempt to use them at the beginning of speeches, a practice found in other interludes. As we have seen, stage directions are usually distinguished by size (Type 4), and they are often preceded by the smallest pilcrows. The location of such directions shows some regular features. In quires A and B and on C1ʳ ten are placed in the margin, but without pilcrows: TLN 82 (A3ʳ, Type 4), 136, 148 (A4ʳ), 158, 164, 177, 178 (A4ᵛ), 227 (B1ᵛ), 408 (B4ᵛ), 464 (C1ᵛ). Putting the directions in the margin was an exacting process as they had to be inserted in the separate column of type otherwise dedicated to speech prefixes. In the same pages of the text there are also some stage directions within the text block: with the exceptions of the large first one at TLN 60 and the anomalous 'ꞩhiꝛper' 609/618, these all follow small pilcrows: 134, 139, 145, 214, 240, 307, 342, 366, 428 (2). After C1ʳ there are no stage directions in the margins: most commonly they are centred, or printed right of centre of the text block, though some are aligned to the right or left margin. From this point onwards, however, we find that the practice of inserting pilcrows becomes irregular and apparently inconsistent: a total of twelve stage directions are placed within the body of the text without pilcrows, while sixteen still have them.

The following table illustrates the distribution of pilcrows in relation to stage directions. The first column shows the number of stage directions within the text having pilcrows, all small except for a large one on A3^r. The second column shows the incidence of stage directions within the text but without pilcrows. The third column shows the incidence of stage directions in margins, none of which have pilcrows.

Outer	with p.	no p.	margin	*Inner*	with p.	no p.	margin
A1^r				A1^v			
A2^v				A2^r			
A3^r	1		1	A3^v			
A4^v			4	A4^r	3		2
B1^r	1			B1^v	1		1
B2^v	1			B2^r			
B3^r				B3^v	2		
B4^v	2		1	B4^r			
C1^r			1	C1^v	1		
C2^v	2			C2^r	1	1	
C3^r	1			C3^v		3	
C4^v				C4^r		2	
D1^r				D1^v			
D2^v		1		D2^r	1	1	
D3^r				D3^v	1		
D4^v	1			D4^r			
E1^r	1			E1^v			
E2^v	2			E2^r	1	2	
E3^r	1	1		E3^v	1		
E4^v				E4^r	2	1	

From this it is clear that initially the practice was to put stage directions in the margins without pilcrows, or to mark them within the text block with pilcrows. After C1^r this practice is changed: no more directions were put into the margins, and in the text block they fall into two categories. These changes may well be significant with regard to the possibility of different compositors. It is especially notable in this respect that after C1^r the more difficult method of putting directions in the column for speech prefixes was abandoned.

Furthermore, these directions in the dialogue column show another note-worthy variation in spacing above and below the line. A stage direction within the main text block was moved during press correction between 609 and 618; this is discussed below. Elsewhere there are two stage directions on dialogue lines within the main text block, both justified right, at 1005 and 1006. The incidence of stage directions within the main text block but on separate lines is as follows:

Space above, no space below: TLN 307, 428.
Space above, space below: TLN 214–15, 240–1, 937.
No space above, no space below: TLN 134, 139, 145, 342, 366, 567.
No space above, space below: TLN 476, 514, 521, 537, 548, 600, 605, 646–8, 776, 807–8, 860, 962, 1016, 1041, 1062, 1084, 1085–6, 1105, 1139, 1140–1, 1150.

There is a significant change of practice at the top of C1ᵛ, TLN 476: up to this point the first three methods are used exclusively, but from here on the fourth is used with only two exceptions. This happens to coincide with the discontinuing of the marginal directions noted above.

All the entrances and exits are marked except for Greedygut's exit at TLN 593. Four of the directions are concerned with costume. Two are for the roles undertaken by Player 4, who was probably a boy playing women's parts: Trust is identified as 'a woman' who is 'playnly' dressed but with a crown (TLN 646–8), and Treasure finely so, also 'a woman' but 'finely apparled' (807–8). Lust enters 'like a gallaunt' (TLN 60), and one stage direction concerns the bridle (1085–6). The steps in the spectacular bridling and release of Inclination are given special attention (TLN 521, 537, 605). There is mention of properties: swords (TLN 134, 240), spectacles (241) and the 'similitude of dust, and rust' brought on by Time to mark symbolically the end of Lust and Treasure (1140–1). There are a number of directions about movement and action which indicate how the actors are to behave: 'Wrestle, and let Luste seeme to haue the better at the firste' (TLN 139); 'Staye and then speake' (145); 'Caste him and let him arise again' (148); 'Bowe to the grounde' (342); 'Gape and the Vile gape' (367); 'Make a going back' (476); 'Struggle two or thre tymes' (514). Two directions indicate a person addressed, at TLN 1005 and 1006, and one requires a mode of speech 'Bragging/ly' (227–8). The 'Pause' at TLN 164 is considered below at p. xxiii.

The outcome of this consideration of the stage directions is that we may have some evidence here of playhouse practice in costume, movement, speech style, and entrances and exits, and we may also have further clues to the determination of the number of compositors. We should notice that the punctuation after the stage directions suffers from inadequacies similar to the punctuation in the text itself.

Apart from the punctuation, there are a number of manifest errors in the printing. It may be that proof reading was not always systematic. The following apology appears in Purfoote's printing of Lewis Evans, *Rebellion of Romishe Prelacie* (1570, STC 10591): 'If there be anye faulte in the Printing, the gentle Reader will beare with mee, for, mine absence at the correcting of somme leafes may excuse it' (E8). A list of apparent errors and possible irregularities will be found in Appendix 1. It will be seen that some appear to be mechanical, whereas others involve misreading or misunderstanding of the copy.

Some aspects of the printing do not match the general competence noted above: damaged individual letters, and the inking of the formes is rather uneven. For the former the most vulnerable letters are the long 's' and the lower case 'd', which tends to become bent in the upper part. Uneven inking, which is particularly noticeable in upper case letters, is interesting because most of the individual irregularities can be seen repeated through all the copies, thus confirming that they are all examples of the same edition. It has also been noticed that some marks and blemishes on individual type run through all the copies as in 'ſtande' (TLN 344, 'ſt' marked) and 'thoſe' (494, 'h' marked).[23] In some instances individual types give the appearance of having been damaged or compressed, suggesting that they were not tightly locked into the formes, as 'h' in 'beholding' (TLN 5), 'd' in 'pounde' (323), and 'r' in 'treaſures' (434).

A shortage of upper case type is implied where initial lower case is used for words at the beginning of lines. Shortage occurs with black letter upper case 'T', 'W', and 'Y' in Type 3:

Outer	T	W	Y	Inner	T	W	Y
A	7		1		1	1	5
B	7	9	5				6
C			1				2
D		3					6
E							2

From this it looks as though a change occurred after the first two quires. This may have been because the supply was improved at that point, though it might be related to different compositors working from different cases. However, the shortage of 'Y' seems to have persisted. Individual lower case sorts also substitute for 'Q' (TLN 22) and 'Z' (569).

One further point may be worth notice regarding these shortages of upper case letters. The shortages are greatest on two pages printed last in their respective formes: A4ʳ (1 T and 4 Y) and B4ᵛ (5 T, 6 W, 3 Y). In respect

[23] In two fascinating instances a hair or some similar piece of debris has become caught on the type and it is possible to work out the order in which the five surviving sheets were printed by noting how it shifts across the face of the letters: these are visible in the facsimile on 'Venus' (TLN 624) and 'Wherein' (862).

of A4^r the shortage is found also on A2^v (7𝕮 and the first 𝔇) but not on A4^v. This suggests that the setting of sheet A may have been by formes, with the inner forme set first. The initial shortage of '𝔇' might have arisen because type was locked in the forme of another book Purfoote had been printing.

It may be that such shortages are in some way related to another feature of the printing. There does appear to be confusion about capitalization for abstract names in the body of the text and this occurs more frequently towards the end of the play. In many instances where a character is clearly intended, the name begins in lower case, as in '𝖙𝖗𝖊𝖆𝖘𝖚𝖗𝖊' (TLN 985), '𝖕𝖑𝖊𝖆𝖘-𝖚𝖗𝖊' (986), '𝖙𝖗𝖊𝖆𝖘𝖚𝖗𝖊' (1000), '𝖕𝖑𝖊𝖆𝖘𝖚𝖗𝖊' (1001), '𝖑𝖚𝖘𝖙' (1008), '𝖙𝖞𝖒𝖊' (1148); conversely when a common noun is intended, it is capitalized, as in '𝕵𝖚𝖘𝖙' (977, 1001). In a few cases the distinction is less than totally clear. I have not listed instances of this type of doubtful reading in Appendix 1.

The only press variant is on C3^v, and it concerns the location of a stage direction:

Sheet C (inner forme)

C3^v	609	𝖂𝖍𝖎𝖘𝖕𝖊𝖗, 𝕾𝖍𝖊] ROS, HN
		𝖂𝖍𝖎𝖘𝖕𝖊𝖗, 𝖜𝖍𝖎𝖘𝖕𝖊𝖗, 𝕾𝖍𝖊] BL, TEX, BOD
C3^v	618	𝖊𝖆𝖗𝖊. 𝖜𝖍𝖎𝖘𝖕𝖊𝖗, &] ROS, HN
		𝖊𝖆𝖗𝖊. &] BL, TEX, BOD

At TLN 609 in BL/TEX/BOD '𝖂𝖍𝖎𝖘𝖕𝖊𝖗' appears in Type 3 and it is repeated using Type 4, and there is a blank space in the middle of 618; in ROS/HN there is a wide blank space in 609, and '𝖜𝖍𝖎𝖘𝖕𝖊𝖗' in Type 4 appears at 618. As the spaces have not been altered in this process it looks as though they may have been so set originally, before '𝖜𝖍𝖎𝖘𝖕𝖊𝖗' (Type 4) was inserted. This suggests that the compositor was initially in some doubt as to where to put the stage direction. It was apparently intended that Inclination should whisper twice to Lust: first to tell him salaciously what pleasures Treasure might afford, and secondly to detail the names of others who also might provide such delights. Of the two versions ROS/HN is nearer to being satisfactory because it makes the stage business clear at 618. One possibility is that prior proof correction was involved. The printer's copy might have read (for instance):

609	Whisper,	She is called Treasure.
618	Yea harke in your eare. / & many other more	Whisper /

As we have seen, the practice of putting stage directions in the margin was discontinued after C1^r and so it would have been desirable to incorporate '𝖜𝖍𝖎𝖘𝖕𝖊𝖗' within the line. Conjecturally, the compositor's first setting would be:

609	𝔚𝔥𝔦𝔰𝔭𝔢𝔯,	𝔖𝔥𝔢 𝔦𝔰 𝔠𝔞𝔩𝔩𝔢𝔡 𝔗𝔯𝔢𝔞𝔰𝔲𝔯𝔢.	
618	𝔜𝔢𝔞 𝔥𝔞𝔯𝔨𝔢 𝔦𝔫 𝔶𝔬𝔲𝔯 𝔢𝔞𝔯𝔢.		& 𝔪𝔞𝔫𝔶 𝔬𝔱𝔥𝔢𝔯 𝔪𝔬𝔯𝔢

This would then have been miscorrected at proof stage by inserting the stage direction in the wrong line, giving the extant uncorrected state:

609	𝔚𝔥𝔦𝔰𝔭𝔢𝔯, 𝔴𝔥𝔦𝔰𝔭𝔢𝔯,	𝔖𝔥𝔢 𝔦𝔰 𝔠𝔞𝔩𝔩𝔢𝔡 𝔗𝔯𝔢𝔞𝔰𝔲𝔯𝔢.	
618	𝔜𝔢𝔞 𝔥𝔞𝔯𝔨𝔢 𝔦𝔫 𝔶𝔬𝔲𝔯 𝔢𝔞𝔯𝔢.		& 𝔪𝔞𝔫𝔶 𝔬𝔱𝔥𝔢𝔯 𝔪𝔬𝔯𝔢

The press correction would then give:

609	𝔚𝔥𝔦𝔰𝔭𝔢𝔯,	𝔖𝔥𝔢 𝔦𝔰 𝔠𝔞𝔩𝔩𝔢𝔡 𝔗𝔯𝔢𝔞𝔰𝔲𝔯𝔢.	
618	𝔜𝔢𝔞 𝔥𝔞𝔯𝔨𝔢 𝔦𝔫 𝔶𝔬𝔲𝔯 𝔢𝔞𝔯𝔢.	𝔴𝔥𝔦𝔰𝔭𝔢𝔯, & 𝔪𝔞𝔫𝔶 𝔬𝔱𝔥𝔢𝔯 𝔪𝔬𝔯𝔢	

But this reading still has the disadvantage of the unfilled gap in TLN 609, perhaps reflecting the initial uncertainty.

THE TRIAL OF TREASURE AND WAGER'S ENOUGH IS AS GOOD AS A FEAST

The remarkable correspondence of some seventy-three lines, by my count, between *Trial* and William Wager's *Enough is as Good as a Feast* [*c.*1570] raises some questions regarding the relationship between the two plays and the possible authorship of *Trial*.[24] The correspondence occurs between *Trial* C4ᵛ–D2ʳ and *Enough* A3ᵛ–B1ᵛ. The corresponding lines are:

Trial	Enough
661–7	121–7
682–93	188–99
697–708	200–11
709–41	220–52
[742–53	253–7 These lines are more divergent.]
754–62	258–66[25]

Though the corresponding passages are in the same order, there are passages in both texts which adjust their material to the respective contexts. Thus in *Enough* extra speeches are found giving scope for the dominating

[24] The correspondence was first noticed by L. B. Wright, 'Social Aspects of Some Belated Moralities', *Anglia*, 54 (1930), 107–48. He thought the direction was from *Enough* to *Trial*.

[25] I have used numeration from W. Wager, *The Longer Thou Livest* and *Enough is as Good as a Feast*, edited by R. Mark Benbow (London: Edward Arnold, 1968). However for the text of quotations I follow the unnumbered, old spelling facsimile: *William Wager: Enough is as Good as a Feast*, with an introduction by Seymour de Ricci (New York: George D. Smith, 1920). In Appendix 3 below the relevant passages in *Enough* are given in facsimile from the unique copy in the Huntington Library.

characterization of Worldly Man, as in *Enough* 149–55, 174–80, and conversely the retrospective reference to the bridling of Inclination at *Trial* 668–74 is omitted in *Enough*. Verbal correspondence is not exact in every line and indeed R. Mark Benbow concludes that only twenty-two lines are the same, though he does not indicate what constitutes the similitude and does not list the lines he has counted.[26] Some of the variations are minute and appear inconsequential, but it should be noted that in both texts the differences are carefully integrated and there is no apparent dislocation.

However, a few of the differences may help to indicate priority and I suggest that the *Trial* version may be the earlier, in line with the sequence of publication: before 1567 for *Trial* and before 1570 for *Enough*. It must be admitted, nevertheless, that this will remain a conjecture as the evidence is not strong and is sometimes ambiguous. The most notable item is the apparent condensation of *Trial* 742–62 into *Enough* 253–66. We might describe this passage in *Trial* as an 'estates' catalogue giving scope in descending order to emperors, potentates and princes (742), then to noble men (749), and finally to poor men and commons (756). These are reduced in *Enough* to ancient famous men (253) and commons (260) and it seems more likely that this is a compression than an expansion. In the light of this it is worth noting that *Trial* ends with verses headed 'Praie for all estates'.

The passage about ambition at *Trial* 731–41 is closely similar in *Enough* and has the same number of lines, but its ending in the latter is a simplifying of the concept:

> God graunt every one of us earneſtly to repent,
> And not to ſet our mindes on this fading treaſure,
> But rather wyſhe and wil, to doe the Loꝛdes pleaſure.
>
> *(Trial 739–41)*

> But God I truſt ſhall diſapoint their intent.
> And overthrowe the power of fading treaſure:
> And cauſe us al to wiſh for the heavenly pleaſure.
>
> *(Enough 250–2)*

It seems also that the allegorical conflict between Lust and Just which is at the heart of *Trial* but absent from *Enough* is consciously referred to in *Enough*:

> Be ye alwaies mindeful to walke in the waies of the Juſt,
> And ad ever moꝛe vertue to your honeſt name,
> And at no hand be over come with covetouſe or luſt.
>
> *(Enough 254–6)*

[26] Benbow, p. x, n. 5.

This passage in *Enough* comes very near the beginning of the play and the ideas in it are therefore available for development as the play progresses.

It should perhaps be added that in some cases the rhythms of lines from *Trial* are slacker in *Enough*, as in the difference between *Trial* 724 and '𝕿𝔬 𝔯𝔢𝔰𝔦𝔱𝔢 𝔱𝔥𝔢𝔪 𝔞𝔩𝔩 𝔦𝔱 𝔴𝔬𝔲𝔩𝔡 𝔟𝔢 𝔳𝔢𝔯𝔶 𝔩𝔬𝔫𝔤' (*Enough* 235), and similarly the loss of 'the' from *Trial* 728: '𝕴𝔰 𝔤𝔯𝔢𝔞𝔱 𝔯𝔦𝔠𝔥𝔢𝔰 𝔞𝔰 𝔴𝔦𝔰𝔢 𝕶𝔦𝔫𝔤 Salomon 𝔡𝔬𝔬𝔱𝔥 𝔰𝔞𝔶' (*Enough* 239). The addition of '𝕯𝔞𝔲𝔦𝔡', *Enough* 121, to *Trial* 661 has a similar effect. Two further considerations may increase the likelihood of the dependence of *Enough*. *Trial* has few local references: two are classical, Troy and Athens, and four English, Salisbury Plain and three in London, Bow-bell, St Paul's and Smithfield. *Enough* has many more London references, making its location there more probable. The greater density suggests addition rather than subtraction. In addition the two interludes share thirteen classical or biblical allusions out of respective totals of fifty-four (*Trial*) and thirty-seven (*Enough*). Ten of the thirteen, nearly one third of the total in *Enough*, occur in the shared passages,[27] whereas the allusions in *Trial* are both more frequent and more widely distributed. That the shared passage is thus more anomalous in *Enough* makes it more credibly the borrower.

If then, there is a flow from *Trial* to *Enough* there arise two useful corrections: '𝔣𝔦𝔡𝔢𝔩𝔦𝔱𝔦𝔢' (*Trial* 700) is corrected to '𝔦𝔫𝔣𝔦𝔡𝔢𝔩𝔦𝔱𝔦𝔢' (*Enough* 203); and '𝔴𝔥𝔢𝔫' (*Trial* 713) is improved to '𝔴𝔥𝔬𝔪𝔢' (*Enough* 224).

Whether or not this direction of changes is accepted, there are also some clues to be found about authorship, for there are some additional features which the two plays have in common outside the correspondence we have been discussing. The most notable of these is the management of the theatrical figure of the Vice. This stage convention had been developing since the 1530s when John Bale and John Heywood first named it, even though their differing examples of the role were not as fully realised as became the custom later. The convention became so popular that it was found to be almost indispensable to writers of interludes in the 1560s and 1570s.[28] Between Inclination in *Trial* and Covetous in *Enough* there are a number of similarities, both of the Vices being named on the title pages. They both begin with an elaborate but nonsensical speech about their adventures and deeds, thus establishing their status in the plays. Both these speeches show that the Vice is to play with conscious reference to the audience. They are

[27] Lines 122, 188–92, 201, 231–4, 239. For allusions and place names see Darryll Grantley, *English Dramatic Interludes: A Reference Guide* (Cambridge: Cambridge University Press, 2004), pp. 92 and 358.

[28] See my 'Deceptions: "The Vice" of the Interludes and Iago' (*Tudor Theatre*, 8 (2009), 105–24). We know of twenty interludes between 1561 and 1576, most of them having a 'Vice': see Alfred Harbage, *Annals of English Drama*, 975–1700, revised by S. Schoenbaum (London: Methuen, 1964).

given to oaths, often with a derogatory Catholic flavour, a feature to which we return below. They become involved in fighting and both have daggers to threaten others. They both indulge in conspicuous laughter. They both play inventive theatrical roles: Inclination plays up as a sort of horse in the two episodes where he is bridled (*Trial* 521–605, 1085–1139) and Covetous seeks to entrap his victim by a copious display of weeping, itself a characteristic of the Vice in other plays (*Enough* 699–710).[29] Though these devices are different, they are set pieces of stage technique which would give scope for the skilled actor who, we assume, usually played the Vice. The details of the Vice's performance are often backed up by explicit stage directions in both texts.

There are other items tending to draw the plays together. These include the behaviour of the lesser vices, who sing part songs of moral import developing the allegories; the use of low class, foolish characters who are belittled; frequent use of classical and biblical allusions and analogues, especially invoking philosophers; the role of Contentation in both and the similarities between the function of God's Visitation and God's Plague.[30] Most particularly there is the device of the divided and contrasted protagonists, Lust and Just in *Trial* and Worldly Man and Heavenly Man in *Enough*.[31] In each case the faulty protagonist is made to pay for his sins while the virtuous one is amply rewarded. There are also some interesting similarities in vocabulary as in '𝔤𝔞𝔭𝔢' *Trial* 366, *Enough* 477; '𝔠𝔲𝔯𝔠𝔥𝔶' *Trial* 324–5, *Enough* 1087 sd; '𝔊𝔬𝔡𝔡 𝔪𝔞𝔫 𝔥𝔬𝔟𝔞𝔩𝔩' *Trial* 498, *Enough* 1353; '𝔞𝔩𝔰𝔬𝔱𝔦𝔞𝔱𝔢' *Trial* 421 (and six more examples), *Enough* 391; and '𝔅𝔶 𝔩𝔞𝔡𝔶' *Trial* 607, *Enough* 835; as well as the apology for the poverty of English rhetoric, *Trial* 56–8, *Enough* 72–3.

In addition there appears to be an ideological similarity between the two plays in the Calvinist stance, manifested in references to the elect, *Trial* 769, 978, *Enough* 221. Both are distinctly Protestant in tone, and the use of Catholic oaths by the Vice reinforces this.[32] One particular allusion within

---

[29] The Vice weeps, usually insincerely, in at least nine interludes, as in Thomas Preston, *Cambyses, King of Persia*, in *Minor Elizabethan Drama (Tragedy)*, vol. 1, edited by Ashley Thorndike (London: Dent, 1910), l. 1126, John Pikeryng, Horestes, edited by Marie Axton, *Three Tudor Classical Interludes* (Cambridge: Brewer, 1982), l. 748 sd, and *Common Conditions*, edited by Roberta Barker, Malone Society Reprints (Oxford: Oxford University Press, 2004), ll. 1275–83.

[30] No other characters of this name are listed in Thomas L. Berger and William C. Bradford, Jr, *An Index of Characters in English Printed Drama to the Restoration* (Cambridge: Cambridge University Press, 1998).

[31] Contrasting paired protagonists appear in fifteenth-century *moralités* but they are rare in interludes.

[32] Both use 'by the mas' (*Trial* 197, *Enough* 403), 'byr lady' (*Trial* 1121, *Enough* 1074), 'Mary' (*Trial* 549, *Enough* 551 and frequently), 'passion of me' (*Trial* 793, *Enough* 883),

the passage in common also supports the Protestant stance. Just comments on how ambitious leaders disdained their brethren '𝕬𝖓𝖉 𝖇𝖚𝖗𝖓𝖊𝖉 𝖜𝖎𝖙𝖍 𝖋𝖎𝖗𝖊 𝖙𝖍𝖊 𝖈𝖍𝖎𝖑𝖉𝖊 𝖜𝖎𝖙𝖍 𝖙𝖍𝖊 𝖒𝖔𝖙𝖍𝖊𝖗' (*Trial* 734; spoken by Contentation at *Enough* 245). This has been traced to a horrific incident involving persecution of Protestants during the reign of Queen Mary which is recorded in John Foxe's *Acts and Monuments*.[33]

To sum up there are notable links between the two plays which ought not to be ignored even if they are not absolutely conclusive of common authorship. If the attribution of *Enough* to the William Wager who became rector of St Benet's Gracechurch on 22 July 1567 and was licensed to preach in any London parish in 1579 is correct, there is a distinct possibility that he was also the author of *Trial*.[34] This would account for the extremely discriminating process by which the passage in common discussed above is so carefully integrated into both plays, irrespective of the question which is the borrower and which the lender. Its integration needs to be related to the creative thinking about how to use allegory which is manifest in both. One might even suggest that the sensitivity and sense of purpose perceptible in the adaptation are just what one would expect of someone judiciously reworking and rethinking his own composition.

THE TRIAL OF TREASURE AND PERFORMANCE

As we have suggested, some features of the *Trial* text may reflect stage practice. The doubling scheme for five players on the title page suggests that the printing may have been undertaken in the hope or expectation of selling to would-be performers[35] but it also reflects careful thought about how to cast the play, as was customary in working out how parts were to be distributed at this period. To a large extent the managing of this aspect of the play must be the work of the author, but it is also possible that necessary modifications might have been introduced by the performers. There is

---

'body of me' (*Trial* 480, *Enough* 393 and frequently). Inclination has 'by my hallydome' (464) and Covetous has 'Sancti Blaci' (383), 'Benedicite' (389) and 'Iesu mercy' (1349).

[33] E. B. Daw, 'Two Notes on *The Trial of Treasure*', *Modern Philology*, 15 (1917–18), 53–5; L. M. Oliver, 'William Wager and *The Trial of Treasure*', *Huntington Library Quarterly*, 9 (1946), 419–29. The latter attributed *Trial* to Wager, but the evidence he adduced was not strong. However, he was followed by T. W. Craik, *The Tudor Interlude: Stage, Costume, Acting* (Leicester: Leicester University Press, 1962), p. 33. A further instance of a Calvinist stance in *Trial* appears in Visitation's reference to God's determination (TLN 999).

[34] The attribution was disputed by E. K. Chambers and W. W. Greg: see my entry for William Wager in *The Oxford Dictionary of National Biography* (Oxford, 2001–4).

[35] It must be admitted, however, that such a niche in the market cannot have been very large statistically.

no evidence here that the doubling is meant to be thematic or that it reflects interaction between the parts that are doubled. Instead it appears to be entirely a practical matter designed to limit the number of actors and to use them as busily as possible. It might also be related to the possibility of a small group of actors going on tour. As will be seen from Appendix 2, the scheme as arranged for five actors on the title page is effective and workable, showing considerable expertise, which is not always the case with such plans printed on title pages.[36] The presence of the doubling scheme may suggest that this play was conceived for an adult company, with one boy, rather than for boy actors in an educational environment. Inclination, the part played no doubt by the leading actor and one full of theatrical possibilities in performance, is on the stage for most of the time. The parts for Player 4 are appropriate for a boy, two of them being female characters appropriately dressed, according to the stage directions. Twice, at TLN 307–409 and 962–1016, all five actors are on the stage at the same time. However, the practice noted by David Bevington whereby groups of virtues and vices could be alternated so that the actors could play in both groups, though it is still discernible, has been somewhat modified.[37] Perhaps in the light of the decision to have two protagonists who will never meet again once the action is under way it was thought desirable to have them onstage together for an initial confrontation at TLN 82–159. The scheme is managed in part by allowing for the stage to be cleared on five occasions, as can be seen from Appendix 2.[38] Such a practice, which is comparatively rare in interludes, may well have given additional time for the actors to change parts and costumes. There may have been a similar concern informing TLN 384. Inclination states that after the song Sturdiness is to '𝔱𝔞𝔯𝔶 𝔱𝔬 𝔣𝔞𝔠𝔢 𝔬𝔲𝔱 𝔱𝔥𝔢 𝔪𝔞𝔱𝔱𝔢𝔯' and the latter does remain alone on stage for a while after the departure of the other actors.

One intriguing direction in the margin at TLN 164 marks a '𝔓𝔞𝔲𝔰𝔢'. There is no knowing whether this was simply an unfilled gap, but it may be relevant to note that in contemporary French plays a 'Pause' (also 'Pausa' in

---

[36] See the discussion in Barker (ed.), *Common Conditions*, p. vi. The doubling scheme for *Enough* is discussed by David Bevington, 'Staging the Reformation: Power and Theatricality in the Plays of William Wager', in Peter Happé and Wim Hüsken (eds.), *Interludes and Early Modern Society: Studies in Gender, Power and Theatricality* (Amsterdam and New York: Rodopi, 2007), pp. 353–80 (370–4), and Appendix I, 379–80.

[37] Bevington suggests that the separation of the protagonists in *Trial* marks a shift towards homiletic tragedy; see his *From 'Mankind' to Marlowe: Growth of Structure in the Popular Drama of Tudor England* (Cambridge, Mass.: Harvard University Press, 1962), pp. 153–5.

[38] Inclination is given the performance initiative for the new starts at TLN 178, 776, and 1086.

Latin) was often a musical interlude or even a fanfare which marked a shift or change of emphasis in the dramatic process.[39]

It was envisaged that there should indeed be plenty of music in the play. All the actors are required to sing in one character or another. Songs are more frequent in the first half of the play, largely because most of them are used to mark entries. The distribution is as follows, the parenthetical numbers being those given for the actors in the doubling scheme:

TLN 60 Entry	Lust (2)
TLN 214 Entry	Sturdiness (1) Lust (2)
TLN 307 Entry	Greedygut (3) Elation (4)
TLN 390	Lust (2) Greedygut (3) Elation (4) Inclination (5)
TLN 649 Entry	Contentation (1) Just (3) Trust (4)
TLN 774 Optional	Contentation (1) Just (3) Trust (4)
TLN 860 Entry	Pleasure (3)
TLN 937	Lust (2) Pleasure (3) Treasure (4) and possibly Inclination (5: cf. TLN 936 where he unhelpfully offers 'either to helpe or stand still')

Apparently it was thought desirable to make the best possible use of the boy actor (4) since he sings in five of the songs.

The focus of the allegory in *Trial* is facilitated by two well-sustained devices: by having two contrasted protagonists, and by the vigorous and symbolic activities of the Vice. On the one hand there is a moral structure which exposes the futility of indulgence in animal appetites.[40] Inclination is the spur for these, especially when he urges Lust to sexual adventures. But he has to be restrained, and this is achieved when Just physically bridles him.[41] The snaffle which controls him is named Restraint (TLN 596). Eventually it is Lust who releases him, as Inclination had foreseen. But another allegory works through the exposure of the impermanence of worldly wealth epitomised here in the character of Treasure. In the end, as in the scriptures, Treasure is consumed by rust. The theme of wealth and the unchristian perversion of it was a popular one in the 1560s, perhaps

[39] For a discussion of this feature in French and Dutch plays, including the Mons *Passion*, see W. M. H. Hummelen, '*Pausa* and *Selete* in the *Bliscapen*', in Elsa Strietman and Peter Happé (eds.), *Urban Theatre in the Low Countries, 1400–1625* (Turnhout: Brepols, 2006), pp. 51–76.

[40] Bernard Spivack, *Shakespeare and the Allegory of Evil* (New York: Columbia University Press, 1958), p. 207.

[41] T. S. Graves notes a fascinating anticipation of this stage device, in which a horse representing the King of France is bridled by Friendship, Prudence and Might in a court entertainment in 1522: 'Some Allusions to Religious and Political Plays', *Modern Philology*, 9 (1911), 545–54.

reflecting economic stress. It had been treated by using the personification Avarice in earlier plays such as *Castell of Perseverance*, where he appears as a Deadly Sin, and *Respublica*, but there does seem to have been an added urgency in the first decades of Elizabeth's reign, prompting plays such as Ulpian Fulwell's *Like Will to Like* (1568), George Wapull's *The Tide Tarrieth No Man* (1576), and Thomas Lupton's *All for Money* (1578). In all of these as well as in *Enough*, there are scenes which show exploitation and economic pressure.[42]

The realisation of these allegories in theatrical terms is reflected, at least in part, in the text. We have noted the stage directions about costume for Treasure and Trust. Further indications come in the dialogue itself. At their meeting Lust accuses Just of being lousy, whereupon Just admits that his apparel is not like Lust's, which he describes as '𝕯𝖎𝖘𝖌𝖚𝖞𝖘𝖊𝖉 𝖆𝖓𝖉 𝖎𝖆𝖌𝖌𝖊𝖉 𝖔𝖋 𝖘𝖚𝖓𝖉𝖗𝖎𝖊 𝖋𝖆𝖘𝖍𝖎𝖔𝖓' (TLN 103), most likely a reference to some sort of extravagant fashion.[43] Greedygut is described as cow-bellied, which Craik plausibly suggests implies padding (TLN 322).[44] Inclination describes God's Visitation as '𝖎𝖑𝖋𝖆𝖚𝖔𝖚𝖗𝖊𝖉' (TLN 997) which Craik similarly suggests may mean he wears a mask.[45] The visual aspects of costuming are sustained by symbolic actions. In the end the unreliability of Treasure and Lust is emphasised by the last words of Inclination, as both are overwhelmed by Time bearing an undescribed '𝖘𝖎𝖒𝖎𝖑𝖎𝖙𝖚𝖉𝖊' of rust and dust (TLN 1140–1). But these words point up the disturbing truth that, like some other examples of the Vice, he is irrepressible. He warns that he will continue to rebel a thousand times even though he is restrained.[46]

ACKNOWLEDGEMENTS

The facsimile text of this edition is reproduced by permission of the Harry Ransom Humanities Resource Center at the University of Texas at Austin, Texas (Pforz. 524). The extract from *Enough is as Good as a Feast* is reproduced by permission of the Huntington Library, San Marino, California (69673). I should like to thank the staff at these libraries, and also those at the Rosenbach Library, Philadelphia, and the Bodleian Library, Oxford University, for their help and consideration. I am much indebted to Professor Richard Proudfoot, President of the Malone Society, for his care and support.

[42] See my 'Wealth in the Interludes' (forthcoming in *Cahiers Élisabéthains*, 77 (2010)).

[43] *OED* disguised, 1b: altered in fashion of dress for the sake of modish display; sundrie, 1: distinct; 4b: with different or mixed elements.

[44] *The Tudor Interlude*, p. 39.   [45] Ibid., p. 52.

[46] Ill Will is similarly irrepressible in *Wealth and Health*, edited by W. W. Greg, Malone Society Reprints (Oxford: Oxford University Press, 1907), ll. 894–5.

¶A new and mery

Enterlude, called the Triall of Treasure, newly set foorth, and neuer before this tyme imprinted.

¶The names of the plaiers,

First, Sturdines, Contentation,
Visitation, Time.
The second, Lust Sapience, Consolation.
The thirde, the Preface, Iust, Pleasure, Gredy gutts.
The fourth, Elation, Trust, a woman, and Treasure, a woman.
The fifth, Inclination the Uice.

¶Imprinted at Londō in Paules Churcheyarde, at the signe of the Lucrece by Thomas Purfoote.

1567.

THOMAS ✦ PVRFOOTE ✦

¶ Doe all thinges to edifie the Congregation.

Iogenes which vsed a barell for his house,
Being fled frō his father to ẏ citie of Athēs,
Cōforted hun self much in beholding ẏ mouse
which desired neither castell nor hold for her
Cōcerning sustentatiō, ẇe made no differēce, (defēce
But eate what soeuer to her did befall,
And touching her apparell, ẇe had least care of all.

This poore mouses propertie noted Diogenes,
Whiche oftentimes also, he would haue in sight,
And though he ware disciple vnto Antisthenes,
yet he learned of the mouse as muche as he might
In the science of Sophy he had great delight,
But concerning his state, and outward condition
The most can declare, if you make inquisition.

On a time he chaunsed accumpanied to be
With Alexāder, which stode betwene him & the sonne
What requirest thou to haue Diogenes(quod he?)
Is there any thing that by me may be done?
I pray thee stande asyde, and make a little roume
(quod Diogenes)that the sunne vpon me may ẇine,
Nought els requier I of that that is thine.

He vsed to saie, that as seruauntes be obedient
To their bodely maisters being in subiection,
Euen so euill men that are not contente,
Are subiectes and slaues to their lustes and affection,
This lesson vnto vs may be a direction,
Which way our inclination to bridle and subdewe,
Namely if we labour the same to eschewe.

A. ii.   Thus

Thus see you howe little this Philosopher estemed
the aboundaunt possessions of this mūdaine treasure
Which yet notwithstanding at these dayes is demed
to be the originall and fountaine of pleasure,
this causeth luste to raigne without measure,
to the whiche men are subiectes, Diogenes doth say,
yet both lost and treasure in time weateth away.

A Philosopher is he that wisedome doth loue,
Which before Pithagoras, wyse men ware named
Nowe Diogenes being wyse, this doth approue
that some mē of this age, ought as fooles to be blamed
For where the one with treasure lack, his life framed
the other trauaile, care, and labour with grediues,
the same by all meanes, to enioye and possesse.

But as Luste with the luster, conuerteth to dusse
And leaueth of force, his pleasaunt prosperitie,
So treasure in time, is turned to ruste:
As S. James in his epistle sheweth the beritle
Hereof we purpose to speake without temerite,
Therefore our matter is named, ẙ triall of Treasure,
Which time doth expell, with all mundaine pleasure.

Both mery and short we purpose to be,
And therfore require your pardon and pacience,
We truste in our matter nothing you shall see,
That to the godly may geue any offence,
Though ẙ style be barbarous, not fined with eloquēce
Yet our Author desireth your gentle acceptation,
And we the plaiers likewyse, with all humilation.

J.E.   Finis,

Ey howe care away let the world paffe
For I am as lufty as euer I was,
In floures I flonfhe as blofomes in May,
Hey howe care away: hay howe care away.

What the Deuill ailed me to finge thus,
I crie you mercy by my faith for entring,
Mofte like I haue ridden on the flyng Pegafus,
Or in Cock Lorrels barge I haue bene a ventringe,
Syng: why I would finge if it were to doe againe,
With Orpheus and Amphion I went to fchole,
What, laddes muft be liuely attending on the traine
Of lady Delectation, whiche is no fmall foole,
Hey rowfe, fill all the pottes in the houfe,
Cufhe man, in good felowfhip let vs be mery,
Looke vp like a man or it is not worth a loufe,
Hey how troly lowe, hey dery dery,
Ha pleafaunt youth and lufty Iuuentus,
In faithe it is good to be mery this may,
For of mans liuing here, there is no point endentus,
Therfore a litle mirth is worth much forow fome fay.

But remember ye not the wyfe mans fentence,
It is better in the houfe of mourning to be
The in the houfe of laughter where foly hath refidēce,
For lightnes with wifedome can not agree
Though many haue pleafure in foolifhe phantafie.
Enfuing their inclination and lufte,
Yet much better is the life of one that is iufte.

A.iii.

Luste.   Sir, in this you seme against me to inuaye,
Juste.   Nothing but reason I thinke I doe saye.
Luste.   Mary you shall haue a night cap for making ŷ reason,
         Frinde haue you not a pece of stockefishe to sell,
         I would you had a dishe of butterd peason,
         By my faith your communication likes me well,
         But I beseche you tell me is not your name Iuste:
Juste.   Yes forsothe.
Luste.   And my name thou shalt vnderstande is lust,
         And according therto I am lusty in deede,
         But I thinke thou haste drunke of Morpheus seede,
         Thou goest like a Drome idory dreaming & drously,
         I holde twenty pounde the knaue is louly.
Juste.   Myne apparell is not like vnto thyne,
         Disguysed and iagged of sundrie fashion,
         Howe be it, it is not golde alwayes that doth shine,
         But corrupting Copper of small baluation
         To horrible besides is thy operation,
         Nothing more odious vnto the Iuste,
         Then the beastly desires of inordinate luste.
Luste.   It is a shamefull thing as Cicero doth saye
         That a man his owne actes would praise & comende,
         Hypocrites accustome thee like daye by daye
         Checking other men, when they doe offende.
Juste.   Yea but it is an harde thing saieth the Philosopher,
         For a foolishe man to haue his maners reprehended,
         And euen at this daye it is come so farre,
         God graunt for his mercy it may be amended.
         For tell a man friendly nowe of his faulte
         Being blasphemy, pryde, or vyle foinication,
         He wilbe as presumptuous as Aman the haulte
         And repaye with reuenge or els defamation.
                                              Thus

                                                        90

                                                        100

                                                        110

                                                        120

Thus fewe men a friendly monition will beare,
But stoutely persiste and mainteine their til,
And in noble mens houses truly I do feare
There are to many haue suche froward will.

   Woundes and hartes who can abyde this,   *Luste.*
Nay ye vyle vylayne I will dresse you therefore,
your lasy bones I pretende so to blisse,
That you shall haue small luste to prate any more.

   Behold the Image of insipient fooles,   *Juste.*
There are not a fewe euen nowe of thy propertie,
Untill you be put into pouerties scholes:
ye will not forsake this folishe insolentie.

   Nay soft, with thee I haue not made an ende.   *Luste.*
     ❡ Drawe out his sworde,
The Just against lust must alwayes contend,   *Juste.*
Therfore I purpose to wrestle with thee,   *Put it vp.*
Who shall haue the victorie, streight waye we shal see.

   When thou wilt by his fleshe: I shal holde the way   *Luste.*
     ❡ Wrestle, and let Luste seeme to haue the better at the firste.
I know that lust vseth not litle to brag: *Juste.*
   Thou shalt find me as mighty as Sampson the strog   *Luste.*
yea the battell of lust endureth long.   *Juste.*
Woundes and fleshe, I was almost down on my back,   *Luste.*
But yet I will wrestle till my bones cracke.
     ❡ Staye and then speake,
   The ende of thy presumption nowe doth appeare,   *Juste.*
yet doe what thou canst I will not lie here,   *Luste.*
No by his woundes you olde doting knaue,   *Casse him*
thinkest thou that lust will be made a slaue,   *and let him*
I shall mete you in Smithfield or els other wheare,   *arise again*
By his flesh and bloud, I will thee not forbeare.

   Not of my power I doe thee expell   *Juste.*
But by the mighte of his spirite that dwelleth in me,
               Inordinate

Inordinate luste with the iust may not dwell,
And therfore may not I accompanie thee.

Luste. Well goodman Iuste, it is no matter,
But in faithe I pretende not with thee to flatter,

Go out, he must driue him out.
Though from thy company departe I muste,
I shall liue in as much welthynes I truste.

Iuste. Where moste wealth is and moste delectation,
There Luste is commonly of moste estimation:

For where as wealth wanteth idlenes doth sla:
But where idlenes is Lust parteth the stake.

Pause. Thus haue you seene the conflicte of ye Iuste,
Which all good men ought to vse and frequent

For horrible are the fruites of inordinate luste,
Whiche in some case resemble Hydra the serpent,

Whose head being cut of an other ryseth incontinent.

So one of Lustes cogitations being cut a way
There ryseth vp an other, yea many we may saye:

It is requisite therfore that euery degree
Against this his lust, both striue and contende,

And though at the first he seeme sturdy to be,

The Lorde will conuince him for you in the ende,

Your cause vnto him therefore holy commende,

Labouring to auoyde all inordinate luste,

Go out, Enter Inclination the Uise.
And to practise in lyfe, to liue after the Iuste.

I can remembre synce Noes ship
Was made and builded on Salisbury plaine,
The same yeere ye weathercock of Paules caught ye pip

Caste him vnder him selfe againe
So that Bowe bell was like much woe to sustaine,
I can remembre I am so olde,
Since Paradise gates were watched by night,

Iust.
And when that Uulcanus was made a cuckold
Among the great Gods I appeared in sight.

Inordinate

May

Nay for all your smiling I tell you true,
No no, ye will not knowe me nowe,
The might on the earth I doe subdue,
tush, if you will giue me leaue ye tell ye howe,
Howe, in good faith I carenot greatly,
Although I declare my dayly encrease
But then these gentle women wilbe angry,
therfore I thinke best to holde my peace:
Nay I beseche you let the matter staye,
For I would not for twenty poūde come in their hādes
For if there should chaunce to be but one dalila,
By the mas thei would binde me in Samsons bands
But what meane I first with them to beginne,
Seing that in all men I doe remaine,
Because that first I remayned euen within,
And after her Adam and so foorth to Caine,
I perceiue by your lookes my name ye would knowe,
Why you are not ignoraunt of that I dare saye,
It is I that doe guyde the bente of your bowe,
And ruleth your actions also daye by daye,
Forsothe I am called Natural inclination
Whiche bred in old Adams fostred bones,
So that I am proper to his generation
I will not awaye with casting of stones,
I make the stoutest to bowe and bende:
Againe when I luste I make men stande vprighte
From the lowest to the highest I doe ascende,
Drawing them to thinges of naturall might.

¶ Enter Luste, and Sturdines, singing
this songe.

¶ Where is the knaue, that so did raue:

B   D

O that we could him finde,
We would him make, for feare to quake
That loute of lobbishe kinde.
　　My name is lust, & let him truste
That I will haue redresse,
For thou and I, will make him flie,
Mine oulde friende Sturdines.

Luste.　　where is nowe that valiaunt Hercules,
For all his bragges he is nowe ronne away?

Sturdi.　By the guttes of Golya, it is best for his ease,
Braggingly For he was moste like for the pottage to paye.

Inclina.　　Cockes soule: what bragging knaues haue we here,
Come ye to conuince the mightiest conquerer,
It was I that before you now doth appeare,
Which brought to confusion both Hector & Alexander:
Looke on this legge ye prating slaues,
I remember since it was no greater then a tree,
At that time I had a cupple of knaues
Muche like vnto you that wayghted on me.

Luste.　　Cockes precious soule, let vs conquer the knaue,

Sturdi.　By his fleshe and sydes, a good courage I haue,
Stande you therfore a litle asyde
And ye shall see me quickely abate the fooles pryde.
　　　　　　¶Drawe out the swearde, make him put it vp, &
　　　　　　then strike him, looke in your spectacles.

Inclina　Naye I dare not I if thou lookest so bigge,
What should suche a Bore fight with a pigge.
Put vp thy swoorde man we will agree,
So lo, doe so much as beate that for mee.

Sturdi,　¶Nay by his harte, then I will you dresse.

Be

Be Good in thine office gentle friend Sturnines,   Inclina.
For though thou and I doe seme to contende,
yet we are, and must be friendes till the ende,
   Come geve me thy hande I beshrowe thy harte,   Sturdi.
Nay you must take all thinges in good parte,   Inclina.
Who standeth yender captaine Luste.
  Yea mary.   Sturdi.
No remedy then to him go I must,   Inclina.
you haue forgot I dare say your old frend Inclinatió
But let vs renew acquaintaùce again for rocks passió
   Why man our acquaintaunce hath bene of olde,   Luste.
I am yours at commaundement therfore be bolde,
For Luste can doe nothing without Inclination,
Chiefly in matters concerning a pleasaunt vocation.
   In dede Luste may be taken for a thing indifferent   Incli.
Except Inclination be ioyned therebuto,
But when that I once haue receaued my entent,
As I will men to worke so commonly they doe,
   Ye haue harde of the combate betwene me & Iust.   Luste.
ye mary, I harde saye that you laye in the dust.   Inclina.
  What saye ye.   Luste.
Neither one worde nor other ye may me truste.   Inclina.
  Of mine honestie my company he bitterly refused,   Luste.
And in wrestling with me he gaue me the foyle,
Saying: that I had my selfe and other abused,
Leading men in perplexitie & maruellous toile.
  By gogs woundes if we had founde him here,   Sturdi.
We should by his fleshe haue abated his chere.
  I perceiue Sturdines thou art no foole,   Incli.
Tell me of felowship where wentest thou to schole,
  What to reade or wrighte.   Sturdi.
Nay to sweare and fight.   Incli.

B.ii.   For

for I thinke thou canſt neither wrrte, reade, nor ſpel,
But in ſwearing and fighting thou doeſt excell.

Sturdi-
nes.
Thou knoweſt that I am ioyned with Luſte,
And Sturdy by nature I am in like caſe,
What let the worlde wag, all can not be Iuſte,
Some muſt Naturall inclination embrace.

Luſte.
All men Iuſte: no, I remember the ſentence of Tully
That noman is Iuſte, that feareth death, pouertie or
which I do feare all & that marueilouſly, (paine,
For fortune is variable I doe perceiue playne,
And notwithſtanding that ſtir poſſeſſed great gaine,
yet when Paule preached of the iudgement daye,
He trembled for feare and bad him go awaye.

Inclina.
Doth ſuch paſſions often trouble your wynde.

Luſte.
Nay not often, but ſometime I doe them finde,
But then to the entent to driue them awaye,
I either go to ſleape, or els to ſome playe.

Sturdi.
By gogs precious harte, euen ſo doe I,
But ſometyme they comber me peſtilently.

Inclina-
tion.
Well maiſter Luſte, ſuch dumpes to eſchewe
My aduiſe and requeſt you muſt nedes enſue,
That is to become diſciple to doctor Epicurus,
And then you ſhall haue myrth by meaſure & ouerplus
Tuſhe, I knowe a cupple companions in ſtore
That ware marueilous mete for you euermore.
I wiſhe you vnto them.

Luſte.
Well then call them in.

Incli.
Here they come each of them in a knaues ſkinne.

¶ Enter Elacion and Gredy gutte.

With luſte to liue is our delight,
In highe eſtate and dignitie,

Seing

280

290

300

Seing that the Iust put vs to flight,
Let them alone in miserie.

   Nay, they be lusty laddes I tell ye.   Sturdi.
What Inclination, me thought I did smell thee,   Elation
Gyue me thy hande oz we forther go.
   Nowe welcome in faith, and Gredy gutte also,   Inclina.
But syrs, are none of you both acquainted with Lust.
   yes that they haue bene both of them I truste,   Luste.
welcome syzs in faithe welcome vnto me.
   By my trothe I am glad your maistership to sce   Elation.
In health and pzosperitie, as pzesently you bee.
   Bom fay zo am I wod all my harte,   Gredy.
This cowe bellied knaue doth come from the carte,   Inclina.
Ise teache you to speake I hold you a pounde,
Curchy Lob curchy, downe to the grounde.
   Che can make curchy well enowe.   Gredy.
Lower old knaue oz yle make ye to bowe,   Inclina.
The great bellied loute me thinke can not bende,
yes so lo, he beginneth now to amende.
   Well syzs, nowe I remember Esopes aduise   Luste.
whiche he gaue to the Samies against king Crassus,
Therfoze it is good to be wittie and wyse,
And being in libertie to kepe me still thus:
I can not abide a life that is dolozous,
And seing that my name is pzoperly Luste,
I hate the conuersation also of the Iuste.
   Well maister Luste, first ioyne you to me Inclinatió Inclina
Next here with Sturdines you must you acquainte
Curne you about and embzace Elation,
And that wealth may encresse without any restraint
Ioine you with Gredy gutte here in our pzesence,
             B. iii.   That

That all these in you may haue prosperous influence.

¶Bowe to the grounde.

Luste. Out alas, what a sodaine passion is this,
I am so taken that I can not stande,
The crampe, the crampe, hath touched me ywis,
I shall die without remedie nowe out of hande.

Gredy. By my matens chese, our maister is sicke.

Inclina. Stande back Nycoll nody with the pudding pricke,
More braines in thy skinne then witte in thy braine,
Such Gredy guttes in faith would be slayne,
This crampe doth signifie nothing in effect
But howe he is bowed by me Inclination,
None of all your councels he will nowe reiecte,
And therefore feare not to make full declaration.

Sturdi. Then feare not the force of these that be iuste,
But labour your selfe to aduaunce and augment,
Be iocound and liuely sithe your name is lust,
And then you shall easely obteine your entente.

Elation. Esteme your selfe alwayes equall with the beste,
And seeke for promotion, power, and dignitie:
It is good when men may liue as they luste,
And vnto the iuste beare hate and malignitie.

Gredy. Or ye must be gredy to catche and to clawe.

Incli. Well said Gredy gutte, as wyse as a dawe,

Gredy. Eate vp at a mouthfull, houses and landes.

¶Gape and the Vise gape.

Incli. Theres a bengeable mouth to,

Gredy. Neuer feare God nor the gouernours lawe,
But gripe gripe gredely all that cometh in your hads,
By the Masse but Hewe Howlet is pestilens witty,
What guttishe gredinesse the horeson can teache
That thou art not erected in faith it is pitie,
As hie as three trees, and a halter will reache.

Mary

Mary syzs, but your councels hath set me on fire.   Luste.
Hey lusty lad, ho w freshe am I nowe,
Leade me Inclination to haue my desire,
And then at thy request I wyll euer bende & bowe.

He that bendeth to folowe his owne inclination,   Incli.
Must nedes liue a wicked and vile conuersation,
But go matster Luste, I will leade you to a place
Where you shall haue pleasure enough in shozt space.

yea, but shall not this company goe chether.   Luste.
yes mary we foure will all go togerher,   Inclina.
But Sturdines shall tary to face out the matter,
If Juste peraduenture against you should clatter.

By the masse, and well said, but first let vs sing,   Sturdi.
I must tune my pipes first of all with dzinking.   Incli.

Tushe what then, I pzaie thee help vs beare a part,   Elation
yes I will sing the trouble with all my harte,   Incli.

Luste shalbe led by inclination
To carnall cogitation,
Where luste is led wholy by me,
He must fall to Cupidite,
For carnall cares shall him assaile,
And spedely they shall preuaile.

I Sturdines will face it out,
In his cause, sturdy stiffe and stoute,
Then Gredy gutte shall make him eate,
Both house & lands, like bzead & meate.

Elation shal puffe him hie
For to aspier aboue the skie,
Then natural and lozdly luste,
Shall with his poure dispise the Juste.

                                 Our

Elation.   Our songe is ended haste thou other in store,
Inclina.   I shall not haue done this halfe houre and more,
          yet I will nowe I remember, come in Luste
          That I go before is but nedefull and iust,
Go out all pou shalbe nowe led by me Inclination
foure.   to reason and talke with Carnall cogitation.
Sturdi.   Is there more vanitie vnder neath the sonne,   410
          Then to be inclined after this sorte,
          well Luste doth now as other haue done,
          yea, and doe daye by daye, esteming it a sporte,
          this Luste is the Image of all wicked men,
          whiche in seeking the worlde, haue all delectation,
          they regarde not God nor his commaundementes tenne
          But are wholy led by their owne Inclination,
          first to inculcate with Carnall cogitation,
          And after to the desier of all worldly treasure,
          whiche alone they esteme the fulnes of pleasure   420
          with Elation or Pride he is also assotiate,
          which puffeth vp his sences with presumption pestilēt
          then Gredy gutte maketh them continually to grate
          On ŷ mock of this world which he thiketh permanēt,
          I sturdines to beare out all thinges, am bent:
          thus see you howe men that are led by their luste,
          Dissent from the vertuous godlie and Iuste.

                         ¶Go out.   ¶Enter Iuste and Sapience,
Saviēce   The aduise of Aristippus haue in your mynde,
          which willed mē to seke such thinges as be permanēt   430
          And not such as are of a banishing kinde
          For the one with the other is not equiualent,
          Be circumspect therefore, forseing and Sapient,
          For treasures here gotten are vncertaine and vaine,
          But treasures of the mynde do continually remaine.
                                                          This

This is the mynde of Musonus also I remembre,　**Iuste.**
Like as presently you haue aduertised me,
For the which I can not but thankefully render,
Such commendations as is requisite to be,
And as your name is Sapience, thus muche I see,
That on heauenly wisedome you doe depende,
And not on as time doth bring to an ende.

　Truthe in deede, & therfore your name being Iuste,　**Sapiéce**
With me and my documentes must be assotiate,
Where contrary suche as are led by their lust,
To incline euill are alwayes appropriate,
They haue not as you haue, battel & combate,
Against the cogitations that inwardly spring,
But rather are obedient vnto the same thing,
And this is the occasion that men are so ambitious,
And so foolishe led by the luste of their braine,
Sometime to couet, sometime to be vicious,
Sometime the councell of the wyse to disdaine,
Sometime to clime till they fall downe againe,
Sometime to vsurpe the possessions of other,
Sometime to disobeye both father and mother.

　Alas what auaileth it ryches to enioye,　**Iuste.**
Though as muche in comparison as Cressus the king,
What helpeth it to haue Helene in Troye,　**Sapiéce**
If the conscience of man continually sting,
Elation and Pride, no commoditie doth bring,
But is often knowen the forerunner of shame,
And the blotte of immortall memorie and fame.

　Nowe by my hallydome it is alone a,　**Enter In-**
Better sporte in my life I neuer sawe,　**clination**
It is trimme I tel you to dauce with Iohn & Ione a:　**the Vice.**
We passe not a point for God nor his lawe,

　　　　　　　　　　　　C　　　　But

17

But Lust is lusty and full of porridge,
Cogitation and he, in one Bed doth lie
When:here is maister Iuste with his cancred corage,
What an olde doting Sapience then I am dressed I,
So often already Iude hath me restrained,
That I dare not entise him any more,
For through Sapience he hath me clerely disdained
That my courage is spent, and I haue no more.

℞axe a going back,

Sapiēce   Nay softe syr we must talke with you or ye go.
Incli na I can not tary at this time the truthe is so.
Iuste.   Nay, there is no remedy with you w e must talke.
Inclina. By the body of me, I holde best that I walke,
          Or els learne to speake language another wh;le,
          And so I may happen the knaues to beguyle.
Iuste.   Turne back or you go, we haue somewhat to say,
Incli.   Non point parla fransois, nonne par ma foy.
Sapiēce   To deceiue vs nowe him selfe he doth prepare,
Incli.   Ick en can ghene englische spreken vor waer,
          Body of me let me go, or els I shall pisse,
          Iwis maister Iuste, you haue loued me or this,
          Therfore nowe be ruled after my councell,
          And godly thinges for your commoditie I shall you tel
Sapiēce   Let him that is Iuste not lightly ensue,
          His vyle inclination and carnall concupicence,
          But let him rather contende the same to subdue,
          And chiefly those that haue knowledge of Sapience,
          Therefore to brydle this luste do your diligence,
          His craftie prouocations vtterly to restrayne,
          That Iust may liue whyle life doth remaine,
Inclina. Good man ho ball speake you in earnest:
          What doest thou saye, shall the Iust brydle me,

No

No, no, brother snappes, doe the worsse and thy best,
I will not be bridled of him nor of thee.
    Seing Sapience consisteth in heauenly document,   Juste.
And that heauenly document consisteth in sapience
To bridle this wretche I can not but consent,
Sithe I of his purpose haue had oft intelligence.
    Yet againe brydle, it doth not preuayle,   Inclina.
I will not be bridled of the best of you both,
See you this gere heres one will make you to quaile,
Stande backe, to kil you maister iust I would be loth
you haue bene so burned and fried of late,
That it were pitte to hurte you any more,
Back I say, or my dagger shall about your pate,
By the masse but I will spryple make your bones sore.
                   ¶Struggle two or thre tymes,
    I will bridle thee beast for all thy bragging.   Juste.
In faith good man Juste, yle holde ye wagging,   Incli.
Nay brother, ye shall finde me a curste colte to bridle,
Nay in faith, better yet I will make thee to struggle.
    Neuer leue him but ensue the councell of sapience.   Sapiēce
Lo nowe I haue brought him vnder obedience.   Juste.
                   Brydle him,
    Not so obedient as thou thinkest me to haue,   Incli.
Nay brother, ye shall finde me a coltishe knaue,
We he, he, it is good for you to holde faste,
For I will kicke and winche whyle thy lyfe doth laste.
    Thou shalt kicke in deede but no victory wynne,   Sapiēce
Neither to conquer the Just to vngodlines nor sinne,
    O yes, O yes, I will make a proclamation,   Incli.
What shall that be?   Juste.
    If ye will geue me leaue then you shall see,   Incli.
O yes, is there any man or woman that hath lost,
                C.ii.   I gam-

A gambolling gelding with a graye tayle,
Let him come to the Crier and paie for his coste,
And he will tell him tidinges without any fayle.

Sapiece   To the entent,that you may him sharpely restraine,
Let him not enioye so muche of the raine.
❡Bridle him shorter.

Inclina   Cockes soule ,nowe the snaffe cutteth my lip,
I would this luberly knaue had the pip,
I shall leape no hedges while this brydle is on,
Out alas, I thinke it will fret me to the bone.   540

Sapiece   Thus should euery man that wilbe called Iuste,
Brydle and subdue his beastly inclination,
That he in the ende may obtaine perfect truste,
The messenger of God to geue sight to saluation.

Iuste.   That truste to obtaine with him I haue struggled,

Sapiece Then let vs departe and leaue this beast bridled.
❡Go out both,

Inclina.   Mary the deuill go with you and his dun dame,
Such horse maisters will make a colte quickely tame,   550
I would he were hanged that this snaffell did make,
It maketh my chappes so shamefully to ake,
ye haue no pitie on me you I se by your laughing,
I care not greatly if I fall to gambolling,
We he,he,he,he,he,come alofte I saye,
Beware the horse heles I auise you,stande awaye,
The raine of my bridle is tied so shorte,
That I can not make you any more sporte,
But though I be bridled now of the Iuste,
I doubte not but I shalbe vnbridled by Luste,   560
And let not Iust thinke but I will rebell,
Althouh he bridle me tenne times all well,
Though nature saith one dome with a croche,

It

20

It will not lie long but incontinent approche,
Euen so, though that I be bridled a whyle,
The Colte will at length the Curser beguyle,

℄ Enter Gredy gutte running and catche a fall,

Gredy. Chill runne I as fast as I can,
zures did none of you zee a man,
Cham zent in haste from my maister Luste,
So that Inclination nedes come to him must.

Inclf. Where is he nowe I praye thee tell me,
Gredy. Why what haue we here Iesus benedicite,
I holde twenty pounde it is Baalams Asse,
Nay tis a Colte, I see his tayle by the masse,

Inclf. Am I a Colte, nay thou liest lyke a knaue,
Somewhat for thy labour nowe shalt thou haue.

Gredy. Ho ball ho, lousy Iade must ye kicke,
Inclina. Who euer sawe suche a desperate Dicke,
Why Gredy gutte, doest thou not knowe Inclinatiō,

Gredy. Body O me, who hath drest thee of that fashion,
Thou arte bridled for byting nowe in deede,
Syra, maister Luste would haue thee make spede.

Inclf. I am bridled I, euen as thou doest see,
Therefore desier him to come and helpe me,
But what is the matter that he for me sente.

Gredy. Mary to gather with Gredines, nowe he is bent,
He hath had long talke with Carnal cogitation,
And is set on fier by the meanes of Elation,
So that he is so lusty he can not abyde.
Therefore one or other for him must be spied.

Inclina. Well Gredy gutte, I praye thee goe and make haste.
Gredy. Tushe, feare not, chill spende no time in waste.

Incli. I had rather then, xl. pence that he ware come,
If I be bridled long I shalbe vndone,

So

So sharpe is this snaffell called restrainte,
That it maketh me sweate I am so faint:
Harke, I heare the voyce of my maister Luste,
Now I shalbe vnbridled shortly I truste.

Enter Luste,   600

Luste.   Cocks precious woundes, here hath bene vilani.
Inclina. Ye, ye they haue vsed me with to much vilanie,
          That old knaue Sapience so counseled Iuste,
          Bu let me be vnbridled good maister Luste.

                          Vnbridle him,

Luste.   Lo now thou art vnbridled, be of good chere,
          By lady I am glad I haue gotten thus cleare,
          But harke you maister Lust, if I may do you pleasure
              Whisper,   whisper,   She is called Treasure.
Luste.   O my harte is on fyre till she come in place.   610
Inclina. O maister Luste, she hath an amiable face,
          A tricker, a trimmer, in faith that she is,
          The goddes of wealth, prosperitie and blisse.
Luste.   But thinke you that this minion long endure shall.
Inclina.   For euer and euer man, she is immortall:
          There be many other, but she exceadeth them all.
Luste.   What be they, haue you their names in store,
Inclina. Yea harke in youre eare.   & many other more
Luste.   Sithe that the apple of Paris before me is cast,
          And that I may deliuer the same where I will,   620
          I would Prometheus were here to helpe me hold fast
          That I might haue a fore witte with me euer still,
          Pallas I consider in science hath skill,
          But Iuno and Uenus, good will doe I beare,
          Therfore to geue the Appull I know not where.
Incli.   Be conciled by me and geue it lady Treasure,
          It shalbe for your comoditie in y end without measur

                                                        For

22

For hauing the company of this minion lasse,
you shall neuer wante the societie of Pallas,
Juno, nor yet the armipotent Mars,

Can not resiste your strengthe be they neuer so fearce
And as for Venus, you shall haue at pleasure,
For she is bought and solde alwayes with Treasure,
She of her power hath whole countries conquered
The most noble chāpions by her hath ben murthered
Acon for her sake was stoned to death,
Tushe, innumerable at this day spende their breath,

Sume hange or be hanged, they loue her so well,
She is the great goddesse, it is true that I tell.

Which way should I worke of her to haue a sight,
I Inclination will leade you thyther right,
But we must haue Gredy gutte and also Elation.

They are at the house of carnall Cogitation.
Whether I would wyshe that we might departe,
I will leade you thether with all my harte.

  Go out. Enter Iust, Trust, a woman playnly,
     and Contentation, knele downe: sing,
     she haue a crowne,

So happy is the state of those,
That walke vpright and iuste,

That thou Lorde doest thy face disclose
By perfect hope and truste.

Their Inclination thou doest stay,
Aud sendest them Sapience,

That they should serue and eke obey,
Thy highe magnificence.

Thou sendest contentation,
That we in thee may rest,   Ther=

Therefore all adoration,
To thee perteineth best.

Juste.

God careth for his as the Prophet doth saye,
And preserueth them vnder his mercifull wynges,
Namely the Juste that his will doe obey,
Obseruing his holy commaundement in all thinges,
Not for our sake, or for our deseruinges,
But for his owne sake openly to declare,
That all men on earth ought to lyue in his feare.

Truste.

Howe God hath blissed you all men may see,
For first at your entraunce you conquered Luste,
Not by your power, but by myght of the deitie,
As all persons ought to doe that be Juste,
Then through Sapience which God did you sende,
You bridled that brutishe beaste Inclination,
And also ordred you with Contentation.

Conten.

Those that are contented with their vocation,
Be thankefull to God, this is a true consequent,
And those that be thankefull in their conuersation,
Can not but please the Lorde God omnipotent,
But those that be sturdie, prowde, and disobediente,
The Ruler of all Rulers will them confounde,
And rote their remembraunce of from the grounde.

Juste.

When Solon was asked of Cressus the king,
What man was moste happie in this vale terestriall,
To the ende he semeth to attrique that thing,
When men be asociate with treasures celestiall,
Before the ende can no man iudge he doth sate,
That any man is happie that here beareth breath,
But then by his ende pretely iudge we may,
Thus true happines consisteth saith he after death.

If

24

If this be a truthe as vndoubtedly it is,
What men are more foolish, wretched and miserable,
Thē those ŷ in these treasures accōpt their whole blys
Being infect with ambition, that sicknes vncurable,
A wicked Adrastia, thou goddes deceiuable,
Thus to plucke from men the sence of their mynde,
So that no contentation, therein they can finde.

The treasure of this worlde we may well compare Truste.
To Circes the witche, with her crafty cautilitie,
Where with many mens myndes so poysoned are,
That quite they are caried into all fidelitie,
They are coniured in deede, and bewitched so sore,
That treasure is their truste, ioye and delight,
True truste is expelled they passe not therefore,
And against contentation, they continually fight.
But though wicked men folowe their lust,
Criyng, on earth is our felicitie and pleasure,
Yet God doth so guide the hartes of the iuste,
That they respecte chiefly the celestiall treasure.

Alas should we not haue that estimation, Conten.
Which God hath prepared for his dere elect,
Should not our myndes reste in full contentation,
Hauing truste in this treasure, most highe in respecte:
S. Paule, when the Lorde so highe did erecte,
Saith: it passeth the sence of our memory and mynde,
Much lesse can our outward eyes the same finde.
And as for treasures which men possesse here
Through fickelnes of fortune, sone fadeth away,
The greatest of renowme and most worthy pere,
Sometime falleth, in the end to mysery and decaie,
Recorde of Dionisius, a king of much fame,
Of the valiaunt Alexander, and Caesar the strong,

D   Recorde

Recozd of Tarquini⁹, which Superbus had to name,
And of Heliogabolos that ministred with wzonge,
If I should recite all, I should stande very long,
But these be sufficient plainely to appzoue,
Howe sone by vncerteutie, this treasure doth remoue.

Iuste.   It is true, therefoze a mynde well contente,
Is great riches as the wyse king Salomon doth say:
We haue seene of late daies this rancar pestilent
Cozrupting our realme, to our great decaie,
Ambition I meane, whiche chiefly did raigne
Among those that should be examples to other,
We sawe howe their bzethzen they did disdaine,
And burned with fire the childe with the mother,
It is often seene that such monsters ambitious,
As spare not to spill the bloud of the innocente,
Will not greatly sticke to become seditious,
The determination of God thereby to pzeuente:
God graunt euery one of vs earnestly to repent,
And not to set our mindes on this fading treasure,
But rather wyshe and wil, to doe the Lozdes pleasure.

Truste.   O ye Emperours, Potētates, ⁊ Pzinces of renowne,
Learne of Iust with truste your selues to associate,
That like as your vocation, by right doth aske ẏ crown
And also due obediēce, being ẏ appointed magistrate,
So rule that at the laste you may be resuscitate,
And raigne with ẏ almightie with perfect cōtinuāce,
Receiuing double crownes foz your godly gouernaūce
ye noble men, whome God hath furnished with fame,
Be myndefull to walke in the wayes of the Iuste,
Adde bertue euermoze to your honozable name,
Fle from loue of Treasure, catche holde of me Truste.

And

26

And then double felicitie, at the laſt you ſhall poſſeſſe,
And in al earthly doings, God ſhal geue good ſucces.
ye pooꝛe men & commons, walke well in your vocation
Baniſhe luſte and deſier, which is not conuenient,
Let truſte woꝛke in you a full contentation,
Conſidering that it leadeth to treaſures moꝛe excellēt
Foꝛ theſe are vncertaine, but they are moſt permanēt:
youꝛ neceſſitie ſupplie with bertue and truſte,
And then ſhall you enioye your crown among ẏ Juſt,

    As J being pꝛoperly nominate Juſte,   **Juſte.**
Am here aſſociate with contentation,
So haue J my whole felicitie in Truſte,
Who ſlumineth mine eyes to ſee my ſaluation.

    Feare ye not, ſhoꝛtly you ſhall haue conſolation,   **Truſte**
Jf J were once growen in you to perfection,
Euen thus goeth it alwaies with ẏ childꝛen of electiō

    J will departe nowe, will ye go with me truſte,   **Juſte.**
yea J muſt alwaies aſſociate the Juſte.   **Truſte.**
A pſalme of thankeſgeuing firſt let vs ſing,   **Conten.**
To the laude and pꝛayſe of the immoꝛtall kinge.

Here if you will: ſing the man is bleſt
that feareth God. &c.

        ¶Go out,   Enter Inclination laughing.

    Luſt (quod he) now in faithe he is luſty,   **Incli.**
Lady Treaſure and he hath made a matche,
He thinketh that J ware marueylous truſty,
Becauſe J teache him to clawe and to catche,
And now a daies amitie doth therein conſiſte,
He that can flatter ſhalbe well beloued,
But he that ſaieth, thus and thus ſaieth Chꝛiſte,
Shall as an enemy be openly repꝛoued.
                          D. ii.   **Friend.**

Friendſhip, yea, friendſhip cõſiſteth now in adulatiõ,
Speake faire and pleaſe the luſt of thy Loꝛde,
I warrante thee be had in great eſtimation,
When thoſe that tell truthe, ſhalbe abhoꝛde,
A vnhappy lingua, whether wilt thou ren,
Take hede I aduiſe thee, leaſt thou be ſhent,
If ye chaunce to tell any tales of theſe gentle women, 790
With fleſhe hokes and nayles, you are like to be rent,
Nay foꝛ the paſſion of me, be not ſo moued,
And I will pleaſe you incontinent againe,
Aboue all treaſures you are woꝛthy to be loued,
Becauſe you do no men deride noꝛ diſdaine,
You doe not contempte the ſimple and pooꝛe,
you be not his minded, pꝛoude and pꝛeſumptuous,
Neither wanton noꝛ wyly you be neuer moꝛe,
But gentle, louing, modeſtie, and vertuous, 800
Beholde howe a lie can pleaſe ſome folkes diet,
O pacifie their myndes marueilous well,
All whyſte I warrant ye, ſo they in quiet,
Howe to pleaſe you hereafter now I can tell,
Harke, I heare Luſte and my lady Treaſure.
They are giuen to ſolace ſinging and pleaſure.

> Enter Luſte and Treaſure a woman,
> finely appareled.

Luſte.   Ah Amoꝛous Lady of bewtifull face, 810
Thou art hartely welcome into this place,
My harte is inclined to thee lady Treaſure,
My loue is inſatiate, it kepeth no meaſure.

Treaſur   It is I maiſter Luſt that will you aduaunce,
Treaſure, it is that thinges doth enhaunce
Upon me ſet your whole affection and luſte,
And paſſe not a poſnt foꝛ the wayes of the Iuſte,

Treaſure

28

Treasure is a pleasure, beare that in mynde,
Both trustly and true ye shall me alwayes finde.
  As trusty as is a quicke ele by the tayle,   *Inclina.*
What Lady Treasure welcome without fayle,
To be better acquainted with you once I truste,   *Luste.*
But I dare not in the presence of my maister Luste,
ye are welcome syr hartely, what be of good courage: *Inclina.*
Drawer, let vs haue a pynte of white wyne & borage.
  Wherefore I praye thee tell,   *Luste.*
Mary me thinke you are not well,   *Inclina.*
  Not well, who can a better life craue,   *Luste.*
Then to possesse suche a lady as I haue:
Is there any wealth not conteined in treasure,
Ah lady, I loue thee in faith out of measure.
  It is out of measure in deede as you saie,   *Inclt.*
And euen so most men loue her at this date:
Oh she is a mynion of amorous hewe,
Her pere in my daies yet I neuer knewe,   *Inclina.*
(Old quod you) I am an olde knaue I tell ye,
Nay, neuer laughe at ye matter, for doubtles I smel ye
She passeth Juno, Ceres, and Pallas,
More beautifull then euer dame Venus was,
Othea in sapience she doth excede,   *Treasu.*
And Diana in dignitie, of whome we doe reade.
What should faire Heleue once named be,
She excelleth all these maister Luste beleue me.
  Howe saye you, is not this an eloquent lad: *Luste.*
That you haue such a seruaunt, truely I am glad.   *Treasur*
  Ha, ha, nowe in deede I can you not blame,   *Inclina,*
For women of all degrees are glad of the same,
They that flatter and speake them fayre,
Shalbe their sonnes, and peraduenture their ayre.

D.iii.   you

Lust. You tolde me of a brother you had lady Treasure.

Treasur yea syr that I haue, his name is called Pleasure,

And seing you enioye me now at your will,

Right sone I am sure he will come you vntill.

Lust. Truly of him I would faine haue a sight,

For because ye in pleasure I haue marueilous delight.

Inclina. Then honestie and profite you may bidde good night.

Lust. What saiest thou?

Incli. I saie he will shortly appeare in sight,

I knowe by his singing, the same is he,

The misbegotten orpheus, I thinke that he be.

¶Enter pleasure singing this song.

O happy eales, and pleasaunt playes,

Wherein I doe delight a

I doe pretende, till my liues ende

To liue still in such plighte a.

Inclina. Maister pleasure I perceiue you be of good chere,

Pleasur What Inclination old lad, art thou here?

Inclina. Yea syr, and lady Treasure your sister also,

Pleasur Body of me, then vnto her I will go,

What sister, I am glad to mete with you here,

Treasur Welcome vnto me mine owne brother dere,

Maister Lust, this is my brother of whome I tolde,

He is pleasaunt and lusty, as you may beholde.

Lust. Gentleman (I pray you) is your name maister Pleasure

Pleasur yea syr, and I am brother to lady Treasure,

Lust. And are you contented to accompanie me,

Pleasur Where as she is resident I must nedes be,

Treasure doth Pleasure commonly proceade,

But the one is with t'other, they haue both so decreed

Inclina. Mary now you are well in deede maister Lust,

This

This is better I trowe then the life of the Iuste,
They be compelled to possesse contentation,
Hauing no treasure but trust of saluation,
But my lady your mistris, my mistris I would saye,
She worketh you may see to kepe you from decaie.

   O madame, in you is all my delight,   Luste.
And in your brother Pleasure, both daye and night,
The triall of treasure this is in deede,
I perceiue that she is a true frende at neede.
For I haue proued her according as Thales doth saye

And I perceiue that her bewtie can not decaye.

   Alwayes with you I wilbe resident,   Treasur
So that your life shalbe most excellent.

   yea syr, and me Pleasure also you shall haue,   Pleasur
So that none other thinge there nedeth to craue,
I will replenishe your harte with delight,
And I wilbe alwayes with treasure in sighte,
But if you desire to enioye me at your will,
My sister you must haue in reputation still,
And then as her treasure is certaine and excellent,

My pleasure shalbe both perfect and permanent,
Credite not those syr that talke that and this,
Saiyng, that in vs twoo consisteth no blisse,
But let experience your mynde euer moue,
And see if all men vs twoo doe not loue.

   Loue, yes they loue you in deede without doubte,   Inclina.
Which shutteth some of the Gods kingdome without:
They loue you so well that their God they do hate,
As time hath declared to vs euen of late,
But he that on such thinges his study doth caste,

Shalbe sure to be deceiued at the laste.

   What doest thou sate.   Luste.

         Of

Inclina.   Of treasure forsoth ye must euer holde fast,
            For if you should chaunce to lose lady Treasure,
            Then fare well in post this gentleman Pleasure.
Luste.   My loue to them both can not be exprest,
            And especially my Lady you I loue best.
Treasur   If ye loue me as you doe professe,
            Be ye sure you shall wante no kinde of welthines.
Pleasur   And if you haue welthines at your owne wyll,
            Then will I pleasure remayne with you still.
Incli.   You are both as constant as snowe in the sunne,
            Which from snow to water through melting doth run
            But worldly wyse men can not conceaue that,
            To honte for suche myse they learne of the cat.
Luste.   My Lady is amorous and full of fauour.
Inclina.   I may say to you she hath an ilfauoured sauour.
Luste.   What saiest thou?
Inclina.   I saye she is louing and of gentle behauiour.
Treasur   And so I will continue still be you sure.
Pleasur   And I in like case whyle your life doth endure,
Luste,   Ah truste treasure, ah pleasaunt pleasure,
            All wealth I possesse nowe without measure,
            And seing that the same shall firmely remayne,
            To helpe me singe a songe, will you take the paine.
Treasur   Euen with all my harte beginne whan ye will.
Incli,   To it, and I will either helpe or stand still.

                    ¶ Singe this songe.

Am not I in blissed case
Treasure and pleasure to possesse,
I would not wishe no better place,
If I may still haue Welthines,

                                                And

920

930

940

32

And to enioye in perfect peace,
　　　My lady lady.
My pleasaunt pleasure ſhall encreaſe
　　　My deare lady,
Helene may not compare to be,
Nor Creſeda that was ſo bright,
Theſe can not ſtaine the ſhine of thee
Nor yet Minerua of great might,
Thou paſſeſt Uenus farre away,
　　　Lady lady,
Loue thee I will both night and day
　　　My dere lady.
My mouſe my nobs and cony ſwete
My hope and ioye my whole delight,
Dame nature may fall at thy feete,
And may yelde to thee her crowne of righte
I will thy body nowe embrace,
　　　Lady, lady
And kiſſe thy ſwete and pleſaunt face,
　　　My dere lady.

¶Enter Gods viſitation.

I am Gods miniſter called Uiſitation,
Which diuers and many wayes you may vnderſtande
Sometime I bring ſickenes, ſometime perturbation,
Sometime trouble and miſery throughout the lande,
Sometime I ſignifie gods wrath to be at hande,
　　C　　　　　　　　　　　　Sometime

Sometime a foreronner of diſtruction imminent,
But an executer of paine I am at this preſent,
Thou inſipient foole that haſt folowed thy luſte,
Diſdaining the doctrine declared by Sapience,
In treaſure and pleaſure hath bene thy truſte,
Which ẙ thoughteſt ſhould remaine euer in thy preſéce
Thou neuer remembzeſt Thales his ſentence,
Who willeth men in all thinges to kepe a meaſure,
Eſpecially in loue to incertaintie of treaſure,
Euen nowe I am come from biſiting the Iuſt,
Becauſe God beginneth firſt with his elect,
But he is ſo aſſociate and comfozted with truſte,
That no kinde of impacience his ſoule can infecte,
Contentation in ſuche ſozte his race doth directe,
That he is contented with Gods operation,
Comfoztably embzacing me his biſitation,
But nowe I am come to bere thee with paine,
Which makeſt treaſure thy caſtell and rocke,
Thou ſhalt knowe that both ſhe and pleaſure is bain,
And that the almighty thou canſt not mocke,
Anguiſhe and griefe into thee I doe caſte,
With paine in thy members continually,
Now thou haſt paine thy pleaſure can not laſte,
But I will expelle him incontinently,

Luſte.   O cockes harte, what a peſtilence is this,
Departe from me I ſaye, hence gods Viſitation,
Helpe, helpe, lady treaſure thou goddes of blis,
At thy handes let me haue ſome conſolation.

Treaſur I will remaine with you be out of doubte,
Incli.   Will ye be packing you ilfauoured lowte,
Uiſita. Preſently in dede from him thou ſhalt not go,
And why, becauſe Gods will hath not determined ſo,
                                                  But

970

980

990

But in time thou treasure shalt be turned to ruste,
And as for pleasure he shall nowe attend on the Iust.

Gogs woundes these panges encrease euer more. **Luste.**
And my littell finger is spitefully sore, **Inclina.**
you will not beleue how my hele doth ake,
Nay let me alone your part I will take, to Uisitatiõ **Treasur**
Be of good comforte whyle I here remaine, to Lust. **Uisita.**
For pleasure and he shalbe parted in twaine,
It is not mete that he should be participate with lust
But rather with the vertuous godly and Iuste.

Remaine with me still maister pleasure I say, **Luste.**
Nay there is no remedy I must away, **Pleasur**
For where God doth sende punition and paine,
I pleasure in no case can not remaine.

I could in like case separate thy treasure, **Uisita.**
But God doth admonishe thee by losing thy pleasure,
℣ Go out Uisitation and Pleasure,

Fare well in the deuils name olde lousy loute, **Inclina.**
That my maister will die I stand in great doubte,
Ho,ho,ho,howe is it with you maister Luste,
By the fleshe of Goliah,yet Treasure is my truste, **Luste.**
Though pleasure be gone,and I liue in paine,
I doubt not but Treasure will fetche him againe.

Yea,that I will feare not & with you remayne. **Treasur**
The propertie of riche men vndoubtedly he hath, **Inclina.**
Whiche thinke with monie to pacifie Gods wrath,
And health at their pleasure to bye and to sell,
Howe is it maister Luste,are you any thing well.

Against this Uisitation my harte doth rebell, **Luste.**
Gogs woundes,shall I still in these panges remaine.

Feare you not maister Lust, I wil helpe you againe **Treasur**
Treasure in phisicke exceadeth Gallenus,
C. ij. **Luste**

35

Tushe there is no phisition but we shall haue with vs,
To the ease of your body they will you bringe,
And therefore I praie you dispaire in nothing,
Put your trust alwayes in me lady treasure,
And I will restore you againe vnto pleasure,
For I am the Goddes that therein hath power,
Which shall remaine perfect vnto the last houre.

Inclina. Yea, yea, maister Luste, be as mery as you may,
Let Treasure be your truste who so euer say nay.

                  ¶Enter tyme.   1040

Time.   The auncient Grekes haue called me Chronos,
Whiche in our vulgar tongue signifieth time,
I am entred in presently for a certainy purpose,
Euen to turne treasure to ruste and to slime,
And Luste which hath long disdained the Iuste,
Ensuing his filthy and vyle inclination,
Shall immediatly be turned to duste,
To the example of all the whole congregation,
For time bringeth both these matters to passe,   1050
As experience hath taught in euery age.
And you shall beholde the same in this glasse,
As a document both profitable and sage,
Both Lust and treasure come foorth with spede
Into the shop of the most mighty God,
There shall you be beaten to powder in dede,
And for your abusion, fele his scourge and rod.

Inclt.   By saint Mary, then they haue made a wise matche,
I pretende therefore to leape ouer the hatche,
Nay let me departe, syrs stop me not I saye,   1060
For I must remayne though both these decaye.

                          ¶Exeunt.

Luste.   Luste from the beginning frequented hath bene

                              Ik

And shall I now turne to nothing for thee.

    Treasure in all ages hath bene beloued,   Treasur
And shall she from the earth by thee be remoued.

    You know that all suche thinges are subiect to time Time.
Therefore me to withstande is no reason nor ryme,
For like as all thinges in time their beginning had,
So must all thinges in time baniche and fade.

    Gogs woundes, let Treasure remaine stil with me, Luste.
Yea let me continue still in my dignitie.   Treasur

    Nay, I must cary you into Uulcans fire,   Time.
Where you shalbe tried vnto the vttermoste,
Seing Lust against Iust did daily conspier,
To dust he shall turne for all his great boaste,
Both of you shall haue one rigorous hoaste,
Come therefore with spede time can not tary,
To the ende of your felicitie I will you carie.

    If there be no remedy then there is no shifte,   Treasur
He must nedes go that is driuen by the Deuils drifte, Luste.
A cocks precious sydes, what fortune is this,
Whether go I nowe, to misery or blis.

Go out.

❧ Enter Iuste, leading Inclination in his
bridle shakled.

    We, he, he, he, he, ware the horse heles I saye,   Inclina.
I would the raine ware lose that I might run away.

    Nay sithe thou wilt not spare against me to rebell, Iuste.
I will not spare by Gods grace thee to brydell,
All men may see howe vile Inclination,
Spareth not to put the Iust to vexation,
Euen so may all men learne of me againe,
Thy beastly desiers to bridle and restraine.

    Mary syr I am bridled in deede as you saye,   Inclina

E.iii.   And

And shakled I thinke for running awaye,
This snafle is sharpe indeede for the nones,
And these shakkels doe chafe my legges to the bones,
And yet will I prouoke spurne and pricke,
Rebell, repugne lashe out and kicke,
We he, in the Jades name are ye so freshe,
¶This gere I suppose will plucke downe your fleshe.

Juste. Nay softe, thou shalt haue a litle more paine,
For somewhat shorter nowe I will tie thy rayne.
    ¶Enter Trust and Consolation.

Truste. Moste blissed and happie I saye are the Juste,
Euen because they restraine their owne Inclination,
Thou therefore that hast made thy treasure of truste,
Beholde, I haue brought thee here consolation.

Juste. Nowe blyssed be God of his mercy and grace,
With all my harte and soule I doe you embrace.

Conso. Consolation is my name euen as Trust hath saide,
Which is ioye or comfort in this life transitorie,
He that possesseth me, is of nothing afraide,
But hath a moste quiet and peaciable memorie,
For I through trust doth shewe thee the glorie,
That God hath prepared for them before hande,
Wherein at the last they shall perfectly stande.

Truste. Receiue this croune of felicitie nowe at this space,
Whith shalbe made richer in the celestiall place.

Incli. Byr lady, I would I had such a gaye croune.

Juste. Nowe praysed be God for this riches of renoune
Felicitie in this worlde the Just doe enioye,
Namely when the Deuill can them not anoye,
The Lordes worke this is, who be praysed for euer,
Who graunte vs in his lawes still to perseuer.

Conso. Amen, amen, God gyue vs delighte,

                In

1100

1110

1120

38

In his holy couenaunt both daye and night.

Our matter is almost brought to an ende,   **Truste.**
Sauing that Inclination in prison must be shut,
Iuste carie him forth that vseth to contende,
And see that surely enough he be put.

That shalbe done shortely by gods grace.   **Iuste.**
What softe I saye, me thinke ye go a shamefull pace,   **Inclina.**
Was there euer poore colte thus handled before,
Fie vpon it, my legges be onreasonablye sore,
Well yet I will rebell, yea, and rebell againe,
And though a thousand times, ye shouldest me restrain.

                 Leade him out.

       ¶ Enter time with a similitude
           of dust, and rust,

Beholde here howe Luste is conuerted to duste,   **Time.**
This is his Image, his wealth and prosperitie,
And Treasure in like case is turned to ruste,
Whereof this example sheweth the veritie.
The triall of Treasure this is no doubte,
Let all men take hede that truste in the same,
Considering what thinges I tyme bringe aboute,
And quenche out the vngodly their memory and fame.

                 ¶ Enter Iuste.

Why, and is Lust and treasure conuerted to this.   **Iuste.**
yea forsothe.   **Time.**

What foolishe man in them would put truste,   **Iuste.**
If this be the finall end of their blisse,
Muche better I commende the life of the Iuste.

So it is no doubte, for they haue consolation,   **Consa.**
Possessing felicitie euen in this place,
I meane through Truste and hope of saluation,
Whiche setteth out vnto vs gods mercy and grace.

                               Let

Truste.   Let all men consider this good erudition, 1160
And not to put confidence in Luste nor Treasure,
By these two examples receiue admonition,
And also of the sodaine banishement of pleasure.

Time.   Remember that time turneth all thinges about,
Time is the touchestone the Iuste for to trie,
But where as lust & treasur in time is come to nought
Iust possessing Trust, remayneth constantly,
So that as I Time hath reuealed their infamie,
So haue I shewed the Consolation and gaine, 1170
That the Iuste shall receiue that iustly doe raigne.

Conso.   We will nowe no lenger trouble this audience,
Sythe somewhat tedious to you we haue bene,
Beseching you to beare all thinges with pacience,
And remember the examples that you haue seene,
God graunte them to florishe liuely and grene,
That some of vs the better therefore may be.
Amen, Amen, I beseche the blyssed trinitie.

Finis.

¶ Praie for all estates.

Ake hede in tyme, and note this well,
Be ruled alwaies by councell.

Learne of the Iust, to leade thy life
Being free from enuie, wrath and strife,
Presumption, pride, and couetousnesse,
With all other vngodlinesse.

Learne of them alwayes to obey
The Lordes preceptes from daye to daye,
That thou maiest walke as he doth wyll,
And labour thy fonde affectes to kill.

Alwayes subdue thy beastly luste,
And in the Lorde put hope and truste,
Bridle thine inclination
By godly conuersation.

The counsell of the wyse embrace,
The fooles aduise doe then deface,
Watche fast and praie with good delight,
That Adam may be killed quite.

That ioy in vs may still encrease,
That God the Lorde may giue vs peace,
That we may be content with Cruste,
To haue our crowne among the Iust.

¶ Finis.

THOMAS PVRFOOTE

¶Imprinted at Londō in Paules
Churcheyarde, at the signe of the Lucrece by Thomas Purfoote.

43

APPENDIX 1

I have suggested some alternative readings in parentheses, incorporating a few from the Dodsley and Halliwell editions. The distribution by quires is shown to indicate the scatter of errors.

A2^v   37 loſt (lust)
A3^v   111 thee (the *Dodsley*)
A4^v   162 ſla (? slake *to rhyme with* stake *163*)
         167 Hybꝛa (Hydra)

B1^r   188 might (mighty *Dodsley*)
         200 euen (Eve *Dodsley*)
B1^v   228 Inclina. (*speech prefix falls between lines, leaving room for SD above*)
B2^r   247 Sturnines (Sturdines)
         263 reaueled (reuealed)
B2^v   281 Stnrdi= (u *turned*)
         289 thar Flix (that Felix)
         302 cupple (cupple of)
         304 you vnto (you were known vnto *Halliwell*)
B3^r   328 yes (Yet *Dodsley*)
B3^v   341–73 (*all the SPs on this page fall below the line*)
         347 matens cheſe (? matin's cheese—*viz.* Greedygut's breakfast)

C1^r   436 Muſonus (Musonius)
         446 incline (incline to)
C1^v   476 Make a (Make as *Halliwell*)
         498 Godd (Good)
C2^r   500 the woꝛſte (*possibly for 'thy worste'*)
C2^v   558 ſpoꝛte (ꝛ *turned*)
         562 Althouh (Although)
         563 croche (? crutche)
C3^v   601 vilani (vilanie 'ɛ' *better in HN, ROS*)
         604 Bu (But)
         607 *lacks SP for* Inclination
         622 ener (u *turned*)
         627 meaſur (*attested form, but spelling possibly imposed by tight line*)
C4^r   632 haue (have her *Dodsley*)
         646 playnly (? 'apparelled' *omitted*)
         654 Aud (n *turned*)
C4^v   684 attriqute (b *turned*)
         689 coeſiſteth (consisteth)

D1^r   700 fidelitie (infidelitie as 'Enough' *203*)
         713 when (whome as 'Enough' *224*)

D2^r 766 **to** (? **o** *wrong font*)

774 **Here . . . ſing** (*Type 2 used for Type 3*)

D2^v 800 **louing, modeſtie** (louing, modeste; loving modesty *Dodsley*, *omitting comma*)

802 **ⴲ** (Or *Dodsley*)

803 **they** (they be *Dodsley*)

D3^r 823 (*lacks SP for* Treasure)

824 (*probably spoken by* Inclination; *but* Treasure *possible*)

839 **Othea** (Other *Halliwell*)

D3^v 861 **eaies** (? daies *perhaps due to foul case*)

877 **proceade** (preceade)

D4^v 912 **In lina.** (**t** *lost*)

924 **honte** (hunt)

931 **truſte** (trusty *Dodsley*)

E1^v 969 **exectuter** (executer)

E2^r 1005–7 (*The two SPs are one line too high.* Inclination, *not* Treasure *probably speaks 1005 to* Visitation. Treasure *speaks 1006 to* Lust, *and* Visitation *speaks 1007.*)

E2^v 1044 **certainly** (certain)

1061 **muſt** (must not)

E3^v 1101–2 (*Juſt begins to speak at* In the jades *Dodsley*).

1122 **this** (? these)

E4^v 1166 **treaſur** (*attested form, but spelling possibly imposed by tight line*)

The following inconsistent spellings are noted:

Frinde 92, frend 255, frende 888

geue 55, 250, 545, 626, 755 (giue in '*Enough*'), gyue 1127

were 183, ware 12, 39, 303, 594, 779, 1088.

APPENDIX 2

THE DOUBLING SCHEME IN *TRIAL*

Player	1	2	3	4	5
1			Preface		
60		Lust			
82		Lust	Just		
160–77			Just		
178					Incl.
214	Sturd.	Lust			Incl.
307	Sturd.	Lust	Greedy.	Elation	Incl.
410–28	Sturd.				
428	Sapience		Just		
464	Sapience		Just		Incl.
549					Incl.
567			Greedy.		Incl.
594					Incl.
600–46		Lust			Incl.
646–776	Content.		Just	Trust	
776					Incl.
807		Lust		Treas.	Incl.
860		Lust	Pleas.	Treas.	Incl.
962	God's V.	Lust	Pleas.	Treas.	Incl.
1017		Lust		Treas.	Incl.
1041	Time	Lust		Treas.	Incl.
1063–84	Time	Lust		Treas.	
1085			Just		Incl.
1105		Consol.	Just	Trust	Incl.
1140	Time	Consol.		Trust	
1150–78	Time	Consol.	Just	Trust	

APPENDIX 3

FACSIMILE OF WILLIAM WAGER, *ENOUGH IS AS GOOD AS A FEAST*, A3^V–B1^V

The line numbers added here correspond with those in W. Wager, *The Longer Thou Livest* and *Enough is as Good as a Feast*, edited by R. Mark Benbow (London: Edward Arnold, 1967).

Which look for no more then wil serue necessitie:
No against a day to come I do prepare,
That when age commeth I may liue merily.

   Oh saith one inough is as good as a feast,
Yea, but who can tel what his end shalbe?
Therfore I count him wurse then a Beast,
That wil not haue that in respect and see.

   As by mine owne Father an example I may take,
He was beloued of all men and kept a good house:
Whilst riches lasted, but when that did slake,
There was no man that did set by him a Louse.

   And so at such time as as he from the world went,
I mene when he dyed he was not worth a grote:
And they that all his substance had spent,
For the value of xij. pence would haue cut his throte.

   But I trowe I wil take heed of such,
They shall go ere they drink when they come to me:
It doth me good to tel the chinks in my hutch,
More then at the Tauern or ale house tobe.

                ¶ Heauenly man.
   God careth for his as the Prophet Dauid doth say,
And preserueth them vnder his merciful wing:
The Heauenly I mene, that his wil do obay,
and obserue his holy commaundements in all thing.
Yet not for our sakes, nor for our deseruing.
But for his owne name sake openly to declare:
that all men heer on Earth ought to liue in his feare.

                VVorldly man.
   This same is one of our iolly talkers,
That prattleth so much of Heauen and Hel:
Oh, I tel you these are godly walkers,
Of many straunge things they can tel.
They passe men, yea Angels they excel,
Sir, are you not called the Heuenly man?
I haue been in your company ere now but I cānot tel whan

                Heuenly man.
   Yes certainly Sir, that is my name,
Unworthy of any such title I do confesse:

                        God

102
110
120
130

God graunt that I may deserue the same,
And that my faults I may amend and redresse.
Therfore now the trueth do o you héer expresse,
Is not the Worldly man your name?

Vvorldly man.

Yea in déd Sir, I am the very same.

Contentation.

From the Heauenly man I cannot be long absent,
Which in Gods promises hath his consolation:
Considering that he alwaies is content,
Patiently to suffer Gods visitation.
For vnderstand you:my name is Contentation.
Whome the worldly man doth mock and deride;
And wil not suffer him once in his minde to abide.

VVorldly man.

This same is the Grandsire of them all,
This is he that will through water and fire:
God reasoning betwixt vs now hear you shall,
For to folowe him he wil me ernestly require,
But he shalbe hanged or he haue his desire.
You are welcome Sir, sauing my quarrel in déed:
You haue reported of me much more then you néed.

Contentation.

Nothing but trueth Sir, certainly I haue said,
Oft times I haue coūcelled you your couetousnes to leue
But my words as fethers in the winde you haue waid,
And stuck to them as Glue to the water doth cleaue.
But take héed the rewarde therof you shall recciue.
Once again I aduertise thée tobe content:
And giue thanks to God for that he hath thée sent.

Vvorldly man.

I pray you be you content for I am pleased,
And meddle you no more with me then I do with you:

Heauenly man.

Tobe angry without a cause, wout mends must be eased
We wilbe more ernest then euer we were now.
Wo (saith our Saniour) to those that are rich,
Which therin onely haue their consolation:

He

He curſeth them not be cauſe they haue much,
but becauſe they receiue it not with contentation.
Building therwith to them ſelues a good foundation, 170
That is to lay héer on Earth treaſure great ſtoꝛe:
to purchace a kingdome that laſteth euer moꝛe.

Vvorldly man.

Paſſion of me maiſters, what would you haue me to doo?
You are fond fellowes indéed as euer I knew:
If I ſhould not take paines, ride, run and go
Foꝛ my liuing, what therof would inſue?
A begger ſhould I dye, maiſters this is true,
Then my wife and childꝛen that I leaue behinde: 180
I fear me at your hands, ſmall reléef ſhould finde.

Heauenly man.

I haue béen yung (ſaith Dauid) and now am olde,
Yet the righteouſe foꝛſaken I neuer did ſée:
Noꝛ their ſéed begging Bꝛead I did not beholde,
Therfoꝛe your minde to the Pꝛophets doth not agrée,
Caſt all thy burden and care (ſaith Chꝛiſte) on me.
And I wil pꝛouide to kéep thée from daunger and ſtrife:
Onely ſéek thou to liue a godly and good life.

Contentation.

When Solon was aſked of Creſſus the King,
What man was moſte happy in this vale terreſtrial: 190
To the end he ſéemed to attribute that thing,
When men be aſſoſiate with treaſures ſeleſtiall.

Vvorldly man.

By the beginning no man can iudge the ſame Solo n dooth ſay,
That any man is happy that beareth bꝛeath:
But yet by the end partely iudge we may,
Foꝛ true happines (ſaith he) conſiſteth after death.

Heauenly man.

If this be true as vndoutedly it is,
What men are moꝛe wicked, wꝛetched and miſerable:
Then thoſe that in riches account their bliſſe,
Béeing infected with Ambition that ſicknes vncurable. 200

Contentation.

The treaſure of this woꝛld we may wel compare,

To

52

To Circes the Witch with her crafty cawtilitie:
Wherwith many mens mindes so poysoned are,
That quite they are caryed to all infidelitie,

   They are coniured so in deed and bewitched so sore,
That treasure is their trust, yea, hope and delight:
Inough serueth them not til that they haue more,
So against Contentation they stil striue and fight.

Heauenly man.

   Though the Worldly man do folowe their lust,
Crying on Earth is our felicitie and pleasure:
Yet God doeth so rule the harts of the Iust,
That their study is, cheefly to get Heauenly treasure.

Vvorldly man.

   Freends I take you bothe for honest men,
I promise you I would be glad to do for the best:
Mary then I take care which way and when,
I may get treasure therewith to liue in rest.

   Oh, me thinks it is a very pleasant thing,
To see a great heap of olde Angels and Crownes:
When I haue store of money I can be mery and sing,
For money as men say winneth bothe Citties and townes.

Heauenly man.

   Alas why should you not haue that in estimation,
Which God hath prepared for his dear elect:
Should not our mindes rest in ful contentation,
Hauing trust in that treasure moste high in respect,
Saint Paule whome the Lord so high doeth erect.

   Saith, it passeth the sence, our memoryes and minde:
   Much lesse can our outwarde eyes the same finde,
   As for the treasure that you possesse heer,
Through ficklenes of Fortune soon fadeth away:
The greatest of renown and moste worthy Peer,
Somtime in the end falleth to misery and decay.

   Recorde of Dionisius a King of much fame,
Of the valiant Alexander, and Ceaser the strong:
Recorde of Tarquinus which Superbus had to name:
And of Heliogabalus that ministred with wrong,
To resite them all it would be very long.

.B.   Ent

Inough is as good as a feast.

But these be sufficient plainly to proue:
How soon and vncertainly riches dooth remooue.

Contentation.

It is true, and therfore a minde wel content,
Is great riches as wise king Salomon dooth say:
For we haue seen of late dayes this canker pestilent
Corrupting our Realme to our vtter decay.

Ambition I mene which cheefly dooth reign,
Amongst those who should haue been example to other:
Yea we see how the Breethern they did disdain,
And burned with fire, the Childe with the mother.

It is often seen that such monstrous Ambition,
As spareth not to spil the blood of the innocent:
Wil not greatly stick to fall to sedition,
The determinations of God therby to preuent,
But God I trust shall disapoint their intent,
And ouerthrowe the power of fading treasure:
And cause vs al to wish for the heauenly pleasure.

Heauenly man.

O you ancient men whome God hath furnished wt fame,
Be ye alwaies mindeful to walke in the waies of the Iust,
And ad euer more vertue to your honest name,
And at no hand be ouer come with couetouse or lust,
But in Gods holy promise put confidence and trust.

And then double felicitie at the last we shall possesse:
And then in all Earthly dooings God shall giue good successe
Ye poor men and commons walke in your vocation,
Banish fond fantasyes which are not conuenient:
Settle your mindes with inough to haue contentation,
Considering that that leadeth to treasures moste excellent,
For these are vncertain, but they are moste parmanent.

Your necessitie apply with treasure, faith and trust:
And you shall haue inough alwaies among the Iust.

Vvorldly man.

And indeed inough is as good as a feast,
Good Lord how your woords haue altred my minde:
A new hart me thinks is entred in my brest,
For no thought of mine olde in me I can finde,

I would

54